Journal Of A Tour Through The Northern Counties Of Scotland And The Orkney Isles, In Autumn 1797 [by J.a. Haldane]

JOURNAL

OF A

TOUR THROUGH THE NORTHERN COUNTIES OF SCOTLAND AND THE ORKNEY ISLES,

IN AUTUMN 1797.

Undertaken with a view to

PROMOTE THE KNOWLEDGE OF THE GOSPEL OF JESUS CHRIST.

Many shall run to and fro, and knowledge shall be increased.
Dan. xii. 4.

EDINBURGH:

PRINTED BY J. RITCHIE.

Sold by J. OGLE, J. GUTHRIE, & G. PEATTIE,
For the Benefit of The SOCIETY for Propagating the
Gospel at Home.

1798.

INTRODUCTION.

THE general attention which has been excited amongft Chriftians to the miferable ftate of the heathen world, muft give pleafure to every one who, knowing the worth of his own foul, has been taught to value the fouls of his brethren. If a Howard be admired for travelling to diftant countries to alleviate temporal diftrefs, to eafe the pain of the prifoner, whom death fhall ere long deliver from his dungeon; how much more fhould we prize the labours of thofe, who, having forfaken their country and friends, are gone to publifh the name of that Saviour who alone can deliver from eternal mifery. Surely Chriftians can have but one wifh on the fubject, that their labours may be abundantly bleffed, and that by their means thoufands may be brought out of darknefs into the marvellous light of the gofpel.

Experience has proved, that the propagation of the gofpel abroad is intimately connected with fimilar exertions at home. It is lamentable to obferve, that, highly favoured as this country has been, fo many are ignorant of the firft principles of religion. There are indeed eftablifhed teachers, and others fupported by various claffes of diffenters, throughout the country; but the prevalence of unbelief and iniquity daily admonifhes us, that fomething more is neceffary. Good men muft be expected to differ as to thofe means which fhould be employed; but that fomething ought to be done, feems to be generally allowed. Even this diverfity of opinion may be overruled for good. Men, according to their various opinions, purfue different plans to attain the fame object, and what one cannot accomplifh is effected by another.

The perfons who undertook the journey of which the following pages give an account, believed that this fcheme afforded the greatest profpect of ufefulnefs in their particular fituation. They found they had leifure and other means to carry the plan into execution; and while they knew that different opinions would be formed refpecting their conduct, they remembered it was to their own Mafter they mult ftand or fall. The unanimous approbation of their brethren would indeed have been highly gratifying, but this they were not fo fanguine as to expect.

Although the oppofition Chriftians muft daily experience, ought not to ftop them in the path of duty, every unneceffary caufe of offence fhould be avoided. It becomes them fairly to ftate the reafons of their conduct, and by every means in their power, to prevent mifapprehenfion. Such is our prefent intention. We fhall explain the principles on which we undertook, and which regulated our conduct in our journey, and endeavour to anfwer thofe objections which, fo far as we know, have been made to the undertaking itfelf, or to the way in which it has been conducted. We may however premife, that we have no expectation of convincing thofe who materially differ from us in their religious opinions. We fhall fhortly give our views of religion, that our readers may judge how far our fentiments agree with their own.—We confider all mankind as being by nature under condemnation, and that none can efcape the wrath to come, but by believing on Jefus Chrift, God manifeft in the flefh, 1 Tim. iii. 16. who his ownfelf bare our fins in his own body on the tree, 1 Pet. ii. 24. We are farther perfuaded, that no man can fay, from a conviction of its truth, that Jefus is Lord but by the Holy Ghoft, 1 Cor. xii. 3. When any man believes this, we confider him as born again, born of the Spirit, without which he cannot fee the kingdom of God, John iii. 3. The means employed by the Spirit in the new birth, we conceive to be the word of God, as it is written in the fcripture, or preached agreeably thereto; for faith cometh by hearing, and hearing by the word of God, Rom. x. 17. We know that thefe fentiments will entitle us to the character of enthufiafts in the opinion of many, having in every age been foolifhnefs to the bulk even of nominal Chriftians. Such will probably find little fatisfaction in the following narrative. We write principally for thofe who agree with us in the great effentials of religion, although we may differ in matters of leffer moment.

The queftion of lay-preaching * has of late been pretty fully difcuffed †. Without entering deeply into the controverfy, we fhall give fome of the reafons which have fatisfied us, that it is not only lawful, but the bounden duty of every Chriftian to preach the gofpel. We would not here be underftood to mean, that every follower of Jefus fhould leave the occupation by which he provides for his family, to become a public preacher. It is an indifpenfible Chriftian duty for every man to provide for his family. But we confider every Chriftian as bound, wherever he has opportunity, to warn finners to flee from the wrath to come, and to point out JESUS as the way, the truth, and the life. Whether a man declare thofe important truths to two or two hundred, he is

---

* We ufe the term *lay-preaching*, not becaufe we acknowledge a popifh diftinction, unfupported by the word of God, but becaufe the term is generally ufed and underftood.

† See Miffionary and Chriftian Magazines.

in our opinion a preacher of the gospel, or one who declares the glad tidings of salvation, which is the precise meaning of the term *preach*.

If it be said, Preaching means teaching in public, we maintain, that every Christian, according to his ability, has a right to do so, although doubtless various reasons may restrain him from exercising that right. None will be bold enough to say, that without a licence a person may not speak * to one of his fellow-sinners about the way of salvation. Should he be asked in a company of a dozen the question put to Paul by the Jews at Rome, " We desire to hear of thee what thou thinkest? for as concerning this sect, we know that every where it is spoken against:" Could any licentiate blame him if he gave an account of the Christian faith, shewing that the general prejudice against true religion was so far from being an objection to Christianity, that it could not be otherwise if the scripture was the word of God, it being there expressly declared, that real Christians must suffer reproach, and that the friendship of the world is enmity with God. He might continue his discourse while they listened in silence, or they might reply and he answer their objections. In either case we should consider him as having preached to the company. It would make no material alteration if the company consisted of fifty or five hundred, or whether they had been called together by the preacher to hear his opinion.

His *right* to do this could no more be questioned than the right of a man to give himself out as a

* Those who would confine the right of preaching to a certain order of Christians, maintain, that preaching is something different from simply declaring the gospel. In Scripture, however, we find it used indifferently with speaking, &c. and applied either to the private or public declaration of the gospel. It is said of the apostles that daily in the temple, and in every house, they ceased not to teach and *preach* Jesus Christ, Acts v. 42. We are informed that Philip began at the same scripture (which the Eunuch was reading), and *preached unto him Jesus*. Acts viii. 55.

teacher in any particular branch of science. From various circumstances the propriety of his conduct might indeed be called in question; but absolutely to deny his right, would not be less absurd than to maintain, in order to secure proper teachers, that no branch of science should be taught without the walls of a College.

Those who allow that an unlicensed man may preach to one or two or ten, would do well to draw the line, and inform us exactly where lay-preaching ends, and where the authority conferred by a licence begins. Distinctions of this kind appear plainly contrary to reason. Now we never find any thing contradictory to found reason in Scripture, but are constantly dealt with as rational creatures. If we are acquainted with any thing valuable, of which our neighbour is ignorant, the law of love requires that we should make it known, and the more essential it is to his happiness, the greater the obligation. If then all men are by nature children of wrath; if there is only one way of salvation, which is clearly and fully explained in Scripture, and with which every Christian must be acquainted, can it be improper to communicate to our neighbours such an invaluable blessing? We ask no licence to supply the bodily wants, or to relieve the bodily pain of our brethren. It is deemed praise-worthy to find out proper objects of charity; and why should we require a licence to inform our brethren of a certain cure for their diseased souls?

Suppose a person had never studied medicine at College, and consequently had got no diploma, but finding the science pleasant, had made himself acquainted with it. He is seized with an epidemical disorder, and obtains relief by applying certain remedies. He immediately offers his assistance to others, and finds the remedy always efficacious. He forces it upon none, but goes from town to town, informing the inhabitants that at a certain hour he will give his advice *gratis* to all affected. When assembled, he warns them of their danger, but desires them not to rest on his opinion. He mentions a book of acknowledged authority among physicians. He informs them that in it they will find the symptoms of their disease described, and a specific cure pointed out, which has never failed of success, and assures them that death will be the certain consequence of rejecting it. He reads passages of this book, and endeavours to illustrate them; he attests the truth from his own experience. What would the Faculty say? Perhaps they would call him a quack, because he had no diploma; but the appellation would be unjust, since he prescribed agreeably to the only proper method of treating the disease. If he desired admittance into the College of Physicians, they might justly say, a diploma is necessary; but surely they could not object to his practising where the people chose to employ him, or at least the corporation-spirit which might lead them to do so, would be universally condemned. Here then is a case in point. Being convinced by experience, that there is but one remedy for the disease of sin, we warn our fellow-sinners of their danger, appealing to a book, generally acknowledged as divine, for the truth of what we say. We advance no new doctrines, and desire our hearers to follow us no farther then we follow the Scripture.

But men, finding that reason and analogy justify lay-preaching, resort to the order which Christ has established in his church, and maintain that the Scriptures give no sanction to preaching without a licence. Let those men shew us, that unlicensed persons are in Scripture prohibited from preaching. If they cannot do this, surely, there is at least a strong probability, that such conduct is not improper.

We are uniformly taught in Scripture, that the Lord will have mercy and not sacrifice; that he prefers the benefit of his creatures to positive or ceremonial observances. Thus he justified David in eating the shew-bread, and his disciples in plucking the ears of corn. He did not condemn those who took their ox or ass out of a pit on the Sabbath; and can we suppose that he would condemn using means to pluck sinners as brands from the burning, although it were not strictly according to order? But this defence is unnecessary in the present case. We do not find in Scripture, that a licence to preach the gospel is neceffary, and, when conducted in the ordinary way, we maintain that it is completely unscriptural. For example, a licenfe is given to preach, and power withheld to difpenfe ordinances. This is totally to reverse the practice of the apostles, who, while they preached the gospel themselves, employed others to baptize. Thus we find Peter, after preaching to Cornelius, and a few of his friends, when he saw the Holy Ghost had fallen upon them, said, Can any man forbid water that these should not be baptized, which have received the Holy Ghost as well as we? and he *commanded* them to be baptized, although it appears he might easily have done it himself, Acts x. 47, 48. Paul declares he had only baptized two persons and one household amongst the Corinthians, although he had been long in that city, and his preaching had been the means of planting the church. The Lord himself did not baptize, but employed his disciples, while he preached to the people. In short, we can find no scriptural ground for preferring the administration of ordinances to the preaching of the word, and yet we see a man first licenfed to preach, after a farther trial ordained, and *then* he may baptize and administer the Lord's supper.

It may alfo be afked, in what manner is a licenfe obtained? A parent determines to make his fon a minifter; he fends him to College. Having a competent knowledge of Latin and Greek, mathematics and heathen morality, he goes for a certain time to the Divinity-hall. He then receives a licenfe to preach, having fatisfied a Prefbytery that he has made fome proficiency in learning, by giving an account of his ftudies, and delivering a certain number of difcourfes. That he is a Chriftian, and has experienced a work of grace on his own foul, is taken for granted, and no wonder; for many of thofe who give fuch licences fhew by their preaching that they confider fuch things as enthufiafm. We would not be underftood to defpife human learning, nor to fay that a minifter may not derive from a liberal education much advantage; but furely, before a man is fent forth to preach Chrift to others, it might be enquired, whether he himfelf feels his need of a Saviour *. We are told his behaviour during his ftudies is known. It may; but he muft be very imprudent if he cannot keep up a fufficiently decent profeffion to get a certificate from fome minifter; fuch a profeffion may be eafily maintained while he feels none of the power of religion.

That ftated paftors fhould be ordained for the work of the miniftry in Chriftian congregations has never been denied, and we ufurp not this office; but it is equally certain, that it is the duty of Chriftians to exhort one another, and if we follow apoftolic practice, this is not confined to private exhortation, Eph. iv. 15. Heb. iii. 13. x. 24, 25. Now if Chriftians may properly exhort and edify one another, and are called fo to do in their religious affemblies, furely they do not take too much upon them, when

---

* We fpeak of what is the practice, not of the rules of the church, which we believe enjoin that a candidate fhould fatisfy the Prefbytery that he feels the power of religion.

they exhort thofe who are altogether ignorant of the Saviour. Chriftians are commanded to hold forth the word of life. They are the light of the world, and fhould let their light fo fhine before men, that others feeing their good works, may glorify our Father which is in heaven. If it be faid, this ought to be by their lives, we cheerfully admit it; but fhould it not alfo be by their converfation, whether public or private? From various caufes, fome Chriftians who are taught of God in the great effentials of religion, may be unable to communicate with clearnefs what they know; but Peter exhorts every one who hath the gift to minifter the fame, as of the ability that God giveth, 1 Pet. iv. 10.

We are told, it is prefumption for any to judge of their own gifts. We do not judge of our gifts; we leave that to our hearers. If we declare the truths of the gofpel, (and no objections on this fcore have been made to the prefent lay-preachers, fo far as we know), in fuch a way that people continue difpofed to hear us, we receive a fufficient teftimony to our gifts to encourage us to proceed.

The cafe of Apollos is an unanfwerable proof that licenfes were not deemed neceffary in the apoftles days. Many attempts have been made to get rid of this inftance. The introductory letter he got from the brethren to thofe of Achaia, has been converted into a licenfe. If this was a licenfe, we had more than one, for we had feveral letters to the Lord's people in different places. But Apollos preached before he had even this, and however he may be fpoken of in our days, he is faid in Scripture, (before his acquaintance with Aquila and Prifcilla), to have been inftructed in the way of the Lord, and to have been fervent in fpirit, Acts xviii. 25. Others have made him one of the feventy; but they received power to work miracles, Luke x. 9. and we do not hear of Apollos having any fuch proof on which to reft his claim as a preacher. Nor can we fuppofe the Lord would have given fuch teftimony to one who was fo imperfectly acquainted with his doctrine. Is it credible, that any of the feventy would fuffer fo many years to pafs, without enquiring about the perfon, by whom he had been fent out? and might he not have heard both of the death and refurrection of Jefus without much trouble? for thefe things were not done in a corner. Others have fuppofed Apollos to have been a licentiate of John the Baptift. This may be ingenious, but is no argument; for we apprehend it would be difficult to prove, that John ever fent out difciples to preach, although we have no doubt but many (among whom was Apollos), preached the doctrine they had heard from him, confirming it by the Scriptures. The apoftle is not afhamed to clafs this lay-preacher with himfelf. "I have planted, Apollos watered." 1 Cor. iii. 6.

We are informed, Acts viii. 1.–4. that the church, i. e. Chriftians, were all fcattered abroad, except the apoftles, and they that were fcattered, went every where preaching the word. Surely it is not probable, that, on this occafion, *all* who preached were licentiates or paftors. We are told then that women muft have preached. We do not think this a fair conclufion, but we have a better opinion of the zeal of the women than to think they did not preach where they could do it with propriety. This they furely might do to thofe of their own fex in private which would certainly have been preaching*. The apoftle mentions fome women who laboured with him in the gofpel, Phil. iv. 3.

The deacons were ordained to take care of the

---

* The Moravians prefer married men for miffionaries, for the benefit of the labours of their wives, who vifit thofe of their own fex, and inftruct them, where jealoufy would prevent the men being admitted. See Inftructions for the Moravian Miffionaries, § 59. &c.

poor, Acts vi. 3. No licenfe to preach is mentioned, yet we find Stephen fhortly afterwards preaching
in the fynagogue, and confounding the Jews. But
we need not wonder that a fpirit of monopoly in
preaching has arifen amongft minifters. The apoftles were not free from it for a time. They had
feen one cafting out devils in the name of Jefus, and
they forbade him. Why? for this weighty reafon,
"He followeth not with us," Luke ix. 49. The
Lord gave a different decifion, and it ftands on record
for our admonition. We cannot help fuppofing this
man knew fomething more of our Lord than his
name, or probably the devils would no more have
obeyed him than they did the fons of Sceva; and if
he knew any thing of the Lord, he would probably
fpeak of him to the people, and thus not only caft
out devils, but preach; and we know not that any
have fuppofed he had privately received licenfe.
His power to caft out devils, it is faid, proved his
warrant. By the fame rule, if it can be fhewn,
that lay-preaching was ever the means of one being
converted, it proves that the perfon by whofe means
that was effected, was warranted to preach, and o-
thers no doubt may follow the example, and make
the experiment, whether their labours may not be
equally fuccefsful. That many inftances might be
brought, in which lay-preaching has been fuecefsful,
we imagine, will not be difputed.

Even under the Jewifh difpenfation, when, by
divine commandment, the moft minute attention
was paid to method and order, we find Eldad and
Medad prophefying in the camp. Jofhua, jealous of
his mafter's honour, and alarmed for the confequen-
ces of fuch a diforderly proceeding, cried out, My
lord Mofes forbid them. How muft he have been
furprifed to hear Mofes fay, Would God that all
the Lord's people were prophets!

When the members of the church of Scotland and the Seceders are fo keen about licenfes, they bring themfelves into an aukward dilemma. They muft either allow, that the founder of their church was a layman, or hold the ordination of a church to be valid, which they, with the facred Scripture, have termed, the mother of harlots and abominations: for except he got a licenfe from the church of Rome, which is very doubtful, John Knox, and others of the Reformation, were unlicenfed preachers. If it be faid this was matter of neceffity, we anfwer, So is lay-preaching at prefent, when thoufands are perifhing for lack of knowledge, when the gofpel of Jefus is almoft unknown in many parts of the country, and little better than heathen morality fubftituted for the doctrines of Chrift.

But " no man taketh this honour to himfelf, but he that is called of God, as was Aaron," Heb. v. 4. This paffage has been preffed into the fervice to fupport the argument againft lay-preaching Whoever takes the trouble to read the paffage in connection, will find the apoftle is not fpeaking of minifters of the gofpel, but of the high prieft. His object is to fhew, that Chrift did not take the honour of the priefthood to himfelf, but was called of God to be an high prieft. Where then the argument in this paffage lies againft lay-preaching, we confefs ourfelves at a lofs to determine. Let thofe minifters who think they have been called of God to the prieft's office, tell us what they, more than other Chriftians, who are all an holy priefthood, have to offer? For every high prieft, taken from among men, is ordained for men in things pertaining to God, that he may *offer both gifts and facrifices for fins*, ver. 1. Let them tell us what refemblance can be traced between a man making application and receiving licenfe to preach from a prefbytery, and Aaron receiving a call to the office of high prieft from God himfelf.

It is not the bufinefs of prefbyteries to give calls, (at leaft they do not exercife it) ; but, after a perfon thinks his call to the miniftry clear, they give him a licenfe. Let any man come before them, however great his gifts and grace, if he has not complied with their rules, neither call nor licenfe will be granted.

The objection to lay-preaching from the abufe which may take place feems to have but little weight. There is no danger of many leaving their trades and becoming preachers. If indeed every itinerant preacher were to be furnifhed with ftipend and a manfe and glebe, the bait which feems to allure fo many ignorant men into the miniftry, we might well apprehend that improper people would enter into the office ; but when men have only to expect fcorn and ridicule, a fuperabundance of lay-preachers need hardly be dreaded. Again, we are told, if the principle be acknowledged, people may preach what doctrines they pleafe, being under no reftraint, and where is the fecurity that they will preach the gofpel. Experience proves, that neither confeffions of faith, nor articles, nor the reftraints under which men are placed, can fecure the preaching of the pure gofpel ; and if laymen go out and preach error, it will only prove that this, like other fchemes, is liable to abufe. We fhould, however, imagine, that thofe who are difpofed to preach error will find no inducement fufficiently ftrong to lead them voluntarily to inftruct men in the principles of their religion, without any profpect of temporal reward. Like other things, preaching will find its own level. Monopolies are as unfavourable to religion as to trade, and Dr Smith's principles, in the Wealth of Nations, will apply to both. Should unfit men engage in the bufinefs, their hearers will either leave them, or they will themfelves tire of the employment. The chaff will thus be blown away, and the wheat (thofe

who love the Lord Jefus and know the value of immortal fouls) will remain.

We fhall juft mention another paffage of fcripture
which has been brought forward againft lay-preaching, Rom. x. 15. " How fhall they preach except
they be fent?" We might afk, who fends licentiates? perhaps the prefbytery; but who fent them to
the prefbytery? It feems they had judged themfelves
qualified for the work before they got a licenfe. Indeed, if they were not, the licenfe would confer no
additional wifdom or gifts. But the fenfe of the a-
bove paffage is altogether foreign to our fubject.
The apoftle is fhewing from the Old Teftament that
the Gentiles were jointly to partake of the bleffings
of the gofpel with the Jews. In this paffage he fhews
that in order to their receiving the promifed bleffing, preachers or miffionaries muft be fent to them.
But men may be fent by the Head of the church, in
a variety of ways. " He gave fome evangelifts, and
fome paftors and teachers," Eph. iv. 11.

Such are fome of the arguments which have fatif-
fied our minds, that we have a right to preach the
gofpel, founded both on reafon and on the word of
God. We formerly hinted, that our fituation in life
enabled us to undertake the journey without interfering with neceffary avocations, and we deemed the
low ftate of religion a fufficient call for us to go to the
high-ways and hedges, and endeavour to compel our
fellow-finners to lay hold on the hope fet before
them in the gofpel. Had we publifhed one or more
books on the fubjects of which we treated in our
difcourfes, no perfon would have found fault with
unlicenfed men acting in fuch a manner. The writings of laymen in defence of Chriftianity have always been confidered as peculiarly important, as
there is lefs ground to fufpect fuch men of intereft-
ed motives; and the clergy are naturally led to refer to fuch writings, when the enemies of the gofpel have afcribed their zeal to ambition and prieft-

craft. Strange! then, if we might not fpeak on fubjects on which we might have written *.

When minifters are fo anxious that laymen fhould be prevented from interfering with what is called clerical bufinefs, they would do well to fet them an example, by abftaining from fecular employments. It is very common for a minifter in the country to engage in the bufinefs of the farmer. This is furely as great a violation of order as it would be for a farmer to preach, but with this difference, the farmer's preaching may be of ufe to others; the minifter's farming can only profit himfelf. When we condemn farming, we do not fpeak of thofe who, in addition to their glebe, rent a fmall piece of ground for the convenience of their family, but of fuch as enter fo deeply into it, that it becomes a bufinefs. This muft undoubtedly tend to diftract the mind, and take up the attention. If a man engage in farming to any extent, he muft either apply diligently to it, or in all probability he will foon be brought into very great difficulties. Rich men may farm for amufement; but when the profits become an object, much attention muft be paid to all the various branches of hufbandry. This bufinefs being fo entirely different from the duties of the paftoral office, and the neceffary ftudies connected therewith, muft have a very bad effect on the mind. Few men can attend to both. There are, we believe, fome inftances of minifters by no means neglecting the duty they owe to their parifh, while they are extenfively engaged in other bufinefs. Thefe are proofs of fingular abilities, but by no means fhew that thofe very men might not be more extenfively ufeful, if the powers they are poffeffed of were directed to one object.

* Lay-preaching, although new in this country, is by no means fo in England. At fome of the academies no licenfe is given. The ftudents preach in villages, &c. When called to the paftoral office, they then receive ordination.

It is faid the ftipends in this country are infuffi-
cient to maintain a large family. This is a libel
upon thofe who fix them; but, fhould this be
granted, it would only prove, that a man having
the profpect of a family ought not to accept of a
fituation which requires the whole of his time and
attention, while it does not afford him neceffary
fupport.

When a perfon however accepts of a ftipend for
difcharging in a congregation the paftoral office, he
virtually acknowledges, that it is adequate to his fupport, unlefs he fpecify beforehand, that he muft endeavour, by fome other means, to make up the de-
ficiency. Without fuch provifion, his time is not
his own; nor has he a right to alienate a part of it
to improve his income. If it be too fmall, he
fhould give it up altogether, become a farmer, and
preach as often as his bufinefs will permit; but if
he receive a certain fum for preaching the gofpel,
for vifiting and catechifing his people, he ought,
according to Paul's exhortation to Timothy, to give
himfelf *wholly* to thefe things, 1 Tim. iv. 15. which
he cannot be faid to do when fo much of his time
and attention is engroffed by a farm. But it will
be found that the ftipends in general are fully fufficient to fupport a family, although certainly they
will not afford to keep up that rank which has been
thought indifpenfible for a minifter. We fhould remember that refpectability does not confift in living
in a particular ftyle. A very poor man, who fup-
ports his family by the fweat of his brow, is more
refpectable than a perfon poffeffed of great riches,
who does not make a proper ufe of them. Mode-
ration and felf-denial, not worldly rank, fhould di-
ftinguifh the minifters of the lowly Jefus *.

* What becomes of minifters who live in towns, whofe ftipends
are often not much larger than in the country, and where living is
alfo dearer? They have neither a farm nor a fhop, and yet they
maintain their families.

Mr Scott, of the Lock hofpital, London, in his practical obfervations on 1 Cor. iv. fays, " It would be ufeful to thofe who imagine that the credit of the miniftry depends, in a great meafure, on their making a creditable, or even genteel appearance, and who emulate the affluent in the expences of their families, to meditate carefully on the fubject before us, that they might be led to conceive of a more excellent way of maintaining the dignity of character becoming the minifters of Him who had not where to lay his head." In another part of his commentary, which we quote from memory, he obferves, That the devil has gained no fmall advantage, by introducing the opinion, that every minifter muft fupport the rank of a gentleman.

We are far from meaning to infinuate that minifters ought not to receive liberal fupport. To this they are entitled, when their flock can afford it; but there is no neceffity for all minifters, any more than others, living nearly in the fame manner. What may be proper for one, is improper for another, whofe income is confiderably fmaller.

One great evil which arifes from the opinion that minifters muft live in a ftyle fuperior to that of their hearers, is, that where people are very poor, they cannot afford a ftipend which is thought fufficient fuitably to maintain a paftor. The apoftle Paul wrought with his own hands, and fupported himfelf, rejoicing in being able thus to publifh the gofpel freely, and to cut off occafion from the enemies of the truth. At the fame time he always maintained his title to live by the gofpel, but we prefume he did not mean by this that he muft live in a way fuperior to thofe by whom he was maintained. Timothy was commanded to beftow the whole of his time on the duties of his office; and, while thus employed, he would no doubt be fupported by thofe among whom he laboured.

It would be thought unbecoming a minifter to keep a fhop in town; but this would not occupy his attention more than a farm in the country, as he might have one or more fhopmen to act under him. But the cuftom has obtained in the country, where the conduct of minifters is not fo much noticed as in towns; and now people are reconciled to a minifter being occupied with a farm, who would exclaim againft his keeping a fhop.

To fay nothing of the temptation to worldly-mindednefs to which a minifter having a farm, attending markets, &c. is liable, it has a bad effect on his people. It often creates jarring interefts. He is confidered as an intruder, and lofes far more refpect by engaging in the fame purfuits with themfelves, than he can gain by almoft any addition to his income. It frequently leads him from one ftep to another, till it completely entangles him in worldly bufinefs, fo that we fee in fome parts of the country minifters acting as factors for the proprietors who do not refide on their eftates. We would recommend to thofe minifters who are fo fond of comparing themfelves with the priefts under the law, to imitate them in being entirely feparated from worldly bufinefs, efpecially as provifion is made for them by the laws of the land in the eftablifhment, and by their people among diffenters; fo that, with the exception of a very few of their hearers, they have in general a larger income than any of the congregation.

If a man in any other line of life, become a preacher, he may lawfully, we apprehend, continue to attend on his bufinefs, but in fuch a cafe his minifterial duties fhould be a labour of love.

Farming is fpoken of as a relaxation from ftudy. Relaxation is furely neceffary; but it might be found in fome other way. The anxiety a farmer muft frequently feel, is more calculated to diftract and fatigue, than to relax the mind. Surely it is

not neceffary by way of exercife ; a minifter
in the country need not want an inducement to
this, if he is difpofed to vifit and converfe with
his people either in their houfes or in the fields.
Minifters in large towns ftand in as much need of
relaxation as thofe in the country ; yet they have
no farms, which fhews it is not abfolutely neceffary. Vifiting of parifhes being fo generally neglected, may be partly owing to the bufinefs of farming. We fhall be glad to fee this fubject difcuffed.
Hitherto it has too little occupied the attention of
Chriftians.

Some do not queftion our *right* to preach, and even
approve of our general defign, while they blame our
conduct in executing it. We hope we can fay we defired to know what the Lord would have us to do. We
afked for that wifdom which is profitable to direct,
and hope we were not permitted to act in a manner unbecoming the character of fervants of Chrift. One
objection made againft us is, that we preached from
texts of fcripture, inftead of giving what is called an
exhortation. We intended to found every thing we
faid on the word of God, and thought that taking a
text was moft for edification. This practice, however, does not exclufively conftitute preaching. We
believe it was formerly the cuftom to fpeak from a
particular fubject, as faith, love, or repentance ; yet
the good men certainly were preaching. But we
are told, this would have removed prejudice. We
heard much about prejudice ; but cannot fay we
met with much on our journey, either among Chriftians or others : nor do we believe our congregations would have been more numerous and attentive,
had we enjoyed all the influence a prefbyterial licenfe
can confer. It would, we believe, have occafioned
more prejudice had we preached without taking a
text. We may add, we were not difpofed to acknowledge that we had not a right to fpeak from the

Scriptures. Had we departed from the common practice, this might have been supposed.

But the principal objection made against us, is, that we attacked the doctrines of particular ministers. We are asked, might you not have preached the gospel, without attacking individuals? In our turn we would ask, was this the method pursued by the Lord and his apostles? Did *he* rest satisfied with declaring the truth, or did he not likewise warn the people against the doctrine of the Scribes and Pharisees? When the ruler of the synagogue found fault with a woman who was healed on the Sabbath, did not the Lord publicly reprove him, " *Thou* hypocrite, doth not each one of you on the Sabbath loose his ox or his ass from the stall, and lead him away to watering?" Luke xiii. 15. Did *he* only denounce woes against sinners in general, or did he not apply them to Pharisees, lawyers, &c.? Did not the apostles warn the churches, in the very strongest terms, against those who preached another gospel, Gal. i. 8. 2 John, 10, 11. The apostle not only warns Timothy against those who had erred concerning the truth, but names Hymeneus and Philetus as false teachers, 2 Tim. ii. 17, 18. He also warns him to beware of Alexander the coppersmith, 2 Tim. iv. 14, 15.; and surely it is more necessary to warn ignorant people, than such an eminent minister of Christ as Timothy, to beware of men who preach doctrines entirely opposite to those of the gospel.

We doubt not that here, as on other occasions, a cry will be raised, these men would make themselves equal to the apostles, or even to Jesus Christ. No ! We disclaim the idea. We are before him as grasshoppers, as the small dust of the balance. How then could we compare ourselves with JEHOVAH? Nor do we pretend either to the gifts, or measure of grace enjoyed by the apostles ; but their writings and our Lord's conduct, ought to regulate our behaviour.

It might with equal juſtice be ſaid, that when the Lord ſays, " Be ye holy, for I am holy," he commands that we ſhould deſire to be equal to himſelf.

Should a perſon go to a country where the plague was raging, and find, that many who gave themſelves out as phyſicians trifled with the caſes of their patients; were building them up in ſecurity in the midſt of danger, and giving them poiſon inſtead of medicine; would it be ſufficient for him to give good medicines, without pointing out the fatal effects of the poiſon which was daily offered them? Should he be deterred, by the oppoſition it would occaſion, from telling the people that theſe men were deſtroying them? Such conduct would be reckoned baſe and cowardly; and where is the difference? In every part of the country, unconverted men are on the brink of deſtruction. We met with miniſters who were trifling with their caſes, leading them to truſt in refuges of lies, and teaching them to put their own ſincere obedience in the place of Chriſt's finiſhed work. If we had only preached the goſpel, many would have heard in that dull ſleepy manner ſo common in many places of worſhip. They might probably have approved both of their miniſter's ſermon and of ours: but when we declared our doctrines to be perfectly oppoſite to thoſe of their miniſters; when we mentioned the exceptionable paſſages of the ſermons we had heard, and ſhewed that they contradicted Scripture; could there be a more probable means of leading them to examine for themſelves?

It has been ſaid, we ſhould have ſpoken to the miniſters in private. This indeed would have been a forlorn hope. At any rate, we could not have ſpoken to them till we had heard them preach; and while we were ſpeaking to one man who would probably have reckoned us inſolent and fanatical, the congregation (to whom we frequently preached as ſoon as the church was diſmiſſed), would have been ſcattered, and we fhould have had no opportunity of fpeaking to the people at all. If the opinion, that we fhould have fpoken to the minifters in private, be founded on that precept, " If thy brother offend thee, go and tell him," we confider this as wholly inapplicable to the prefent cafe. That precept refpects only our brother in Chrift ; for we cannot imagine the Lord would have directed any but a Chriftian to be carried before the church, Mat. xviii. 17. Now, we can never acknowledge a man as a Chriftian brother who perverts the gofpel of Chrift. Befides, this rule only regards perfonal and private offences. When a fin or offence is open, we are directed to proceed in a different manner. We have both apoftolic precept and example in Scripture for publicly reproving open offenders, 1 Tim. v. 20. " Them that fin, rebuke before all, that others alfo may fear." 1 Cor. v. 4, 5. Gal. ii. 14. " When I faw that they walked not uprightly, I faid unto Peter before them all," &c. But it is afked, what are the poor people to do when they have no opportunity of hearing the gofpel : Should they ftay from church altogether ? They have Mofes and the prophets, Jefus Chrift and his apoftles, and we hefitate not to fay it would give us pleafure to learn, that the hearers of every minifter, whofe fermons we condemned as unfcriptural, had left him. They had much better ftay at home than go to church, and hear error. They might meet together for reading the Scriptures and prayer ; and furely few who know the gofpel will fay that they would not be better employed than in hearing another gofpel. We always warned them of the obligations of Chriftians not to forfake the affembling of themfelves together on the firft day of the week. In many parts of the country they might hear found doctrine among the Seceders, and we care not, if Chrift

be preached, whether it be by Paul, Apollos, or
Cephas.

But an objection is brought againſt men leaving
their pariſh-churches, from the conſideration that
our Lord and his apoſtles attended the ſynagogues.
We may obſerve, that the Jewiſh church was completely different from any modern one. It was
of Divine eſtabliſhment, and therefore, however
great its corruptions, no man might leave it. Thus
the prophets, while they ſo often teſtified againſt the
idolatry of the Jewiſh church, did not attempt to eſta-
bliſh a purer one. The time then was, when men
were to ſacrifice and worſhip God at Jeruſalem, but
that time is no more. Except the church of Rome,
we know of none which pretends excluſively to divine
eſtabliſhment. The true church is not to be found
in one ſect or denomination, but ſcattered among
all who have heard the goſpel. The caſes then of
the Jewiſh church and of any modern one, are by no
means parallel. If they were, how could the Reformation be vindicated ?—Our Lord it is true went
into the ſynagogues, but for what purpoſe? To
teach and inſtruct the people. The Scriptures
were read in the ſynagogues, and even ſtrangers
were allowed to ſpeak from them, and to exhort the
people, Acts xiii. 15. Our Lord and his apoſtles would
ſurely never loſe ſuch an opportunity for preaching
the goſpel. But would he have ſuffered the Scriptures to be wreſted or perverted in his preſence?
Would he have ſuffered the Scribes to explain away
and make void the law of God by their traditions, and
have held his peace: The idea is abſurd. Counte-
nancing ſuch meetings, the principal deſign of which,
as far as we know, was to read the word of God,
was very different from going to hear men who take
a portion of Scripture for a motto to a diſcourſe in
which they expreſsly contradict the doctrines of the
goſpel. Were it the cuſtom in our pariſh-churches

C

for private Chriftians to fpeak, it would be an important duty to attend, even where the gofpel is not preached, in order to declare the truth, and to point out the errors of thofe who teach for doctrines the commandments of men, and exprefsly contradict the word of God. But as this cannot be done, may we not follow the example of Paul, who continued to attend and to preach the gofpel in the fynagogue at Ephefus for three months, but when he found many hardened in unbelief, he left them, and feparated the difciples, Acts xix. 9. The old difpenfation was paft, and the kingdom of God was come. Chriftians were delivered from the bondage of legal ceremonies, and worfhipping in particular places, and they ufed that liberty wherewith Chrift had made them free.

If it be the duty of Chriftians to attend their parifh-churches at all events, what becomes of our Lord's precept, " Beware of falfe prophets," Matth. vii. 15. How are we to beware of them? Is it fufficient to guard againft their doctrines, while we continue to hear them? The Lord has taught us to pray, lead us not into temptation; but if we go every Sabbath to hear doctrines far more agreeable to our corrupt nature, than the pure and humbling doctrines of the gofpel, are we not putting ourfelves in a very dangerous fituation? But we do not argue from probability alone. Our Lord on one occafion warns his difciples againft going forth to fee and to hear falfe prophets, Mat. xxiv. 26. and we do not find encouragement from Scripture to adopt the practice on any occafion. The apoftle's words, 2 John, 10, 11. are exprefs, " If there come any unto you, and bring not this doctrine, receive him not into your houfe, neither bid him God fpeed: for he that biddeth him God fpeed, is partaker of his evil deeds;" and do we not bid a man God fpeed, or, in other words, give him countenance, by continuing to hear him? Suppo-

fing we fhouldget no harm ourfelves, are we not mif-
leading the ignorant, if we attend where error is
preached? When we expect no inftruction, we
are at leaft lofing our time. If we fee the dangerous tendency of the doctrines, and ftill fit with
feeming attention, pretending to join in the prayer
of a man whom we cannot efteem a Chriftian, and
in whofe prayers are fentiments directly oppofite to
our own, what is this but a folemn mockery of
God? Should we fend for a phyfician to our houfe,
and lead others to think we were confulting him,
whilft we were fo fatisfied of his ignorance, that we
would not truft ourfelves in his hands, fhould we be
blamelefs, if others, relying on our fuppofed opinion of his fkill, fuffered from his mifmanage-
ment? The cafes are fimilar, except that in the one,
only the bodies of our brethren could fuffer, but in
the other we might be the means of deftroying both
foul and body.

We can affure thofe who blame our conduct refpecting the minifters againft whom we teftified, that
it was the moft unpleafant fervice we performed on
the journey; and nothing but the confideration of
its being an important duty could have induced us
to go through it. We could have no private end
in view, and would ferioufly requeft our Chriftian brethren who differ from us in opinion to re-
confider the fubject. How would they have advi-
fed us to have acted? Should we have ftaid away
from church altogether, thus expofing ourfelves to
the charge of difregarding public worfhip? or fhould
we have heard fermons openly contradicting the gofpel, without taking notice of what we had heard?
In this way fhould we not have bidden falfe teachers God fpeed, by pretending to join in the worfhip.
Thus indeed we fhould have efcaped oppofition, but
we could not have maintained a good confcience.

We can only fay that it is our earneft prayer

that thofe minifters whofe doctrines we condemned, may be led to fearch the Scriptures, and that
they may receive the Spirit of wifdom and reve-
lation in the knowledge of Chrift.   We fincerely defire to fee minifters throughout the country fo
faithful and laborious, that lay-preaching may become lefs neceffary.

Another very ferious charge brought againft us,
is, that we endeavoured to difturb the peace of the
country.   We know that preaching the gofpel has
always had the effect of difturbing that falfe peace
in which the god of this world defires to keep his fubjects. Thus the Lord tells us, he was not come to fend
peace on earth, but a fword, Mat. x. 34. although he
preached the gofpel of peace. In anfwer to any charge
of a feditious nature, we can only fay, " We fpake
publicly, in fecret we faid nothing." Let it be proved, that our fermons, or private converfation,
were political or feditious, and we refufe not to fuffer the punifhment we deferve.   Our aim was not
to make politicians, but Chriftians.   The fubjects
on which we difcourfed were more important than
politics, in as much as eternity is more important
than time.   It is worthy of remark, that fedition
has been from the beginning a charge againft Chriftians.   The Lord himfelf was faid to be a ftir-
rer up of the people, Luke xxiii. 5. Paul was called a peftilent fellow, and a mover of fedition, Acts
xxiv. 5.; Elijah a troubler of Ifrael, 1 Kings xviii.
17. Our political creed is fhort.   We hold ourfelves
bound to be fubject to the powers that be, not only
for wrath, but for confcience-fake : To render to all
their dues, tribute to whom tribute is due, cuftom to
whom cuftom, fear to whom fear, honour to whom
honour : To pray for kings, and all in authority ;
and to lead quiet and peaceable lives, in all godlinefs and honefty.

Some find fault with our preaching in the ftreets,
and giving intimation by drums, &c. We found by

experience, that although fome pious people might be offended by fuch conduct, yet we had by far the moft numerous congregations in the open air; and befides, when we preached in a meeting-houfe, we found the bulk of the congregation were fuch as heard the gofpel regularly. Our defign was not fo much to preach to Chriftians as to thofe who knew not the gofpel; and we are perfuaded, more were attracted by curiofity than were kept away by prejudice. Our ftay in moft places was necef-farily fhort, and it would have been very difficult to have collected a congregation in any other way than by the hand-bell, or drum. Many idle peo-ple were thus collected, and furely we could not hefitate between perhaps hurting the feelings of a few individuals, and lofing an opportunity of preaching Chrift, to carelefs finners who probably would not have taken the trouble to enter a church. We have to acknowledge the goodnefs of God that we met with fo little interruption and that fo much external decency was maintained by our hearers. Surely the precept, not to give offence to our brother, does not apply here; it only refpects things indifferent. Had it been applied to fchemes of ufefulnefs, hardly any would ever have been adopted; for in almoft every cafe they have at firft given offence even to Chriftians.

Some have blamed us for ftaying too fhort a time in one place. It muft be obferved our time was li-mited, and we are ftill of opinion that it was more advantageous to make an extenfive circuit, by which we might attain a general knowledge of the ftate of religion in the North, and likewife let the people throughout the country know what exertions were making by Chriftians to fpread the knowledge of the Saviour at home and abroad. In future itine-rancies, it may probably be found advantageous to take in a fmaller tract of country, that the labourers may have an opportunity of spending a longer time in one place.

These are some of the objections brought against us. We have endeavoured fairly to meet them. Whether we have answered them in a satisfactory manner, it is not for us to determine. We are fully perfuaded in our own minds, that, amidst many imperfections, we were, upon the whole, in the path of duty; and here we cannot but make a remark, applicable not only to our own case, but to many other schemes of ufefulnefs, That it would better become Chriftians, where they have every reafon to believe that their brethren are actuated by proper motives, to throw a vail of love over the errors of their conduct, than to endeavour to weaken their hands, by leading in the cry raifed againft them by the world. We mean not to claim any particular indulgence for ourfelves. But while we give full credit for uprightnefs of intention to thofe who confider the meafures of their brethren to be dangerous and diforderly, we cannot approve their feeming defire to throw a flur on the whole of their conduct.

A more pleafing tafk now remains for us, gratefully to acknowledge the kindnefs of many of our brethren in Chrift during our journey. To name particular places where this kindnefs was fhewn, would be injuftice to others. We fhall only fay, we hope never to forget the affection we experienced for the fake of Jefus, and we are fully warranted to exprefs our confidence, that he will richly overpay fuch labours of love. Thefe were fometimes more agreeable to us from being unexpected. Where we were taught to look for bigotry, we frequently experienced the greateft liberality and affection; and "we would therefore bear witnefs of their charity before the church." This could not but lead our minds to contemplate that glorious day of gofpel-light, which we truft has begun

to dawn, when Chriftians fhall agree to differ in leffer
matters, and fhall cordially embrace in the arms of
Chriftian affection all who hold the head. Oh that all
might more largely partake of the Spirit of Chrift,
and fay one to another, " Let there be no ftrife, I
pray thee, between me and thee ; for we be brethren."

It gave us much uneafinefs to fee, that in every
place more was not done for the good of fouls, even
by the Lord's people. We hardly found an inftance of
that zeal which leads many minifters and others in England to go to the neighbouring towns and villages,
proclaiming the joyful found, where the gofpel is
not preached *. Surely this would not difgrace
the minifterial office. Had minifters acted in this
manner, the ftate of the country might have been
very different. We mean not however to reflect
on the paft, but to ftir up our brethren for the
time to come. Even among the Seceders, minifters too often content themfelves with preaching
on the Lord's day to their own people, while thoufands are perifhing in the neighbourhood for lack
of knowledge. They may fay, let them come to us :
Our wandering about would not be according to order. Had the apoftles ftaid at Jerufalem, and faid fo,
what would now have been our fituation ? The Lord
hath faid, " Go to the high-ways and hedges, and
compel them to come in." Let not minifters be afraid
left they degrade themfelves by obeying that com-
mand, becaufe laymen are now preaching. Chriftians of every defcription fhould always keep in mind
the faying of our Lord, He that humbleth himfelf

---

* We are well aware, that this does not arife from want of zeal
alone, but from the order eftablifhed by the Seceders, as well as
the National Church. But furely the order appointed by the great
Head of the church is calculated to encourage, and not to prevent
meafures for roufing carelefs finners. The order of any church
that prevents fuch exertions is the ordinance of man. If the Englifh diffenters are diforderly, in this refpect, we wifh to fee a little of fuch diforder in this country.

shall be exalted. Many excuses may be found, such as the prejudices entertained against Seceders, &c. But has the attempt been made? At first there may be prejudice, and the hearers few; but perseverance, by the blessing of God, will overcome prejudice. A minister might preach in some of the places in his neighbourhood two days in the week without interfering with parochial duty, or encroaching too much on the time, for that study which is so necessary to enable any person rightly to divide the word of God. Should ministers act in this manner, there is no danger of their losing the regard due to those who labour in word and doctrine; but if by their conduct they appear to others to be seeking their own ease and dignity more than the Redeemer's honour, they have much reason to apprehend they will soon lose that respect to which they have been accustomed, and which has in many instances arisen from a little of the leaven of priest-craft operating upon ignorance and superstition, and not from that discriminating regard due only to faithful ministers of Christ. The Lord put his disciples in mind, that he had been among them as one that served, and surely the servant is not greater than his master. Let not then his ministers in the present day be ashamed to imitate his example, and that of one who was not a whit behind the chiefest of the apostles, who, though he was free from all men, yet made himself servant unto all, that he might gain the more, 1 Cor. ix. 19.

Some doubts have been expressed as to the propriety of publishing this journal. We do not expect by the publication much worldly honour. But we desire to bear testimony to the Lord's faithfulness in that promise, " Lo I am with you always, even unto the end of the world." He hath given us that support and assistance which he knew to be necessary. May he give us more and more a deep and abiding sense of our vileness, and of our utter unworthiness to be employed in his service. We also publish it, that, by a view of the low state of religion in many parts of the country, and of the willingness of the people to hear the gospel, others may be excited and encouraged to undertake similar journies.

We cannot conclude without seriously calling upon our Christian brethren to confider, whether they are obeying or neglecting their Lord's commandment, "Occupy till I come." Are they doing their utmost to spread the fame of Jesus? Knowledge of the truth and opportunity are surely sufficient calls for them to testify to others the gospel of the grace of God. Whether they have opportunity of doing so to many or to few, let them heartily embrace it, and let them not be terrified though some of the sons of Levi should say, Ye take too much upon you. An inspired apostle informs us, that if Christ was preached he would rejoice, although it were done of envy and strife: and surely he would much more have rejoiced, if men, to whom their brethren can impute no such motives, had preached Christ without a licenfe from men. Let Christians remember who has said, " Whosoever shall do and teach men his commandments shall be called great in the kingdom of heaven."

To thofe who think we should have been more regularly feparated for the work, we can only fay, we wanted no commiffion or authority, but we had the prayers of many of our brethren. We are persuaded we experienced the benefit of these prayers; and now we requeft, that they would join in grateful praifes to the Lord for his goodnefs towards us. May the feed fown yield an abundant harveft, and may his abundant grace, through the thankfgiving of many, redound to the glory of God.

We should have been happy to have given a more full account of the ftate of the country; but the shortnefs of our ftay in moft places prevented this;

and we wifhed as much as poffible to avoid giving
hearfay intelligence. From what we have faid, the
wretched ftate of the country in refpect of religion,
and the neceffity of Chriftians ufing the utmoft exertions, may be feen. Would God that while his
judgments are abroad on the earth, the inhabitants
thereof might learn righteoufnefs ; that both rich
and poor in this country might be humbled under
the mighty hand of God, might hear him in his
providence calling on them to repent, and to bring
forth fruits meet for repentance. This would indeed be a token for good ; but while fo much vice
and impiety prevail in the land, there is too much
reafon to fear the execution of that awful threaten-
ing, " Shall I not vifit for thefe things, faith the
Lord, fhall not my foul be avenged on fuch a nation
as this ?"

Let the Lord's people cry mightily to him to blefs
the attempts which have been made, and are ftill making, to fpread the knowledge of Jefus throughout
the world. Let their utmoft exertions accompany
their prayers, that the time may foon come, when
" the earth fhall be full of the knowledge of the
Lord as the waters cover the fea." ·

JA. HALDANE.
J. AIKMAN.
J. RATE.

P. S. Since writing the above, we are told, that
we have been accufed of preaching againft eftablifh-
ments. We neither preached for nor againft them,
but endeavoured to preach the gofpel. We generally mentioned that when at home we heard the
gofpel in the eftablifhed church ; and when we knew
that in any place they enjoyed a faithful gofpel miniftry in the eftablifhment, we warned the people a-
gainft mifimproving fo high a privilege. It is impoffible for us to guefs at all the objections made againft
us ; but we have ftated them fairly, and endeavoured to anfwer them fully, fo far as we knew them.

We have had occafion to mention in our journal, that we diltributed pamphlets as we went along. As it is poffible their tendency may be mifreprefented, we have fubjoined a lift of them, that the public may have an opportunity of examining their contents. The lift may alfo be ufeful to thofe, who are defirous of occafionally endeavouring to call the attention of their fellow-men to the great concerns of eternity. The pamphlets may be had very cheap, and by the bleffing of God, this may be a means of awakening fome carelefs finners, who neither hear the gofpel in public nor in private. Chriftians would do well to provide themfelves with a few fuch tracts when walking in the fields, or going on a journey. A perfon may be induced to read what he gets from a ftranger, who would not take that trouble, if given him by a pious relation. The time is fhort; fouls are perifhing; and Chriftians ought to embrace every opportunity of warning their brethren to flee from the wrath to come.

Lift of Tracts diftributed.

Short Sermons,	2000
Three Dialogues between a Minifter and one of his Hearers on the true Principles of Religion,	2000
Addrefs to Strangers,	4000
Affectionate Addrefs on the Importance of Religion,	3000
Friendly Advice to all whom it may concern,	5000
An Account of the Converfion of a Negro,	2000
Poor Jofeph,	2000
Affectionate Addrefs to young Chriftians,	150
Regulations for Sabbath Schools, copied from the Miffionary Magazine for May 1797.	250

Copies of the above may be had at the Printing-Office of J. Ritchie, Head of Blackfriars Wynd.

ERRATUM.

P. 39. l. 23. *for* Mark xv. 16. *read* Mark xvi. 15, 16.

JOURNAL, &c.

July 12. LEFT Edinburgh, (after frequent, earneſt and united prayer to God for direction and ſupport), and arrived at North-ferry, where we immediately began our labours. Preached in a ſchoolroom to about fifty perſons. Came forward to á village, called Keltiebridge, about ten at night. Sent an intimation through the neighbourhood, that there would be ſermon next morning at eight o'clock. A congregation accordingly aſſembled of nearly a hundred perſons to whom we preached in the open air. Saw here an old man an Antiburgher, who aſked what commiſſion we had for preaching, and quoted, " How ſhall they preach except they be ſent ?" We told him our views and motives. He ſaid he wiſhed us well, but would give us no countenance. It was very well, he ſaid, to ſend miſſionaries abroad, but that they had no need of any ſuch there. In the morning, however, after we had preached, he ſaid he would have attended, had he not been dull of hearing, and promiſed us his prayers. We then left this place, and came forward the ſame evening to Perth.

July 14. Preached in the hoſpital at Perth. Came on to Scoon, where we preached at the crofs to a very attentive congregation about 2 o'clock, and then proceeded to Cupar, where we preached to upwards of 200 perſons in the Maſon's hall at nine o'clock, the weather not permitting us to preach without, and not having heard of this place fooner. Preached in the fame place next morning, and diftributed pamphlets. A man came to us after fermon apparently much under the power of temptation. He had been fo, we were informed, for a year and a half. He was accompanied by one who feemed to be under the influence of the truth, a hearer of the Methodifts.

July 15. Came on to Meigle, and preached to about 70 people in the church-yard, who feemed very carelefs. Came to Glamis, where we intimated fermon by the hand-bell. A congregation of about 200 people affembled, who heard with much attention. We were here informed, that Kerrymuir was much in need of the gofpel. Accordingly we determined to fpend next day, (being the Lord's day), in that place, rather than at Forfar, as we had intended. Arrived in Kerrymuir about nine o'clock; and although the Lord's fupper was to be difpenfed next day, we found a large market-place quite crouded with idle people. We informed them, there would be fermon next morning at eight o'clock, and in the evening, which at once feemed to excite furprife and derifion. They treated us, however, with more refpect, on our giving them fome pamphlets, and fome of them followed us into the inn, with a view of learning who we were, and what were our intentions.

Lord's day, 16. Preached in the morning at eight o'clock in the market-place to upwards of 200 people. Went to church, and heard fermon. The minifter preached from 1 John iii. 8. The fermon did not appear to us glad tidings to finners. The object of it was to fhew, that the Son of God came into the world to inftruct and enable men to deftroy the works of the devil. He reprefented the gofpel as a contract between God and man, of which the

equitable condition, he faid, was repentance and fincere, although imperfect obedience, which God, he
added, was too juft and too good not to accept. As
he read the fermon, and repeated every paffage of
the fmalleft importance, it was impoffible for us to
miftake the meaning of any of them. The Lord's
fupper was then difpenfed: And it furely muft
affect the minds of all who know the importance
of the gofpel, and the value of mens fouls, to
learn that immediately afterwards, upwards of
1500 perfons, daily acquiefcing in fuch doctrine as
has been mentioned, profeffed to commemorate the
death of Chrift. We heard one table ferved by
a neighbouring minifter. This perfon, to guard
the communicants againft the commiffion of fin,
told them, that if they fell into any after that day,
there remained no more facrifice for them. How
fuch a fentiment could be reconciled with the indif-
criminate admiffion that prevails in that quarter, as
in many others, we leave others to judge. Had
much fatisfaction in hearing an Antiburgher minifter preach in the afternoon. When the eftablifhed church was difmiffed in the evening, we went to
the top of a walled ftair in the market-place, which the
congregation had to pafs, and immediately began as
ufual by finging. There might probably be near
1000 people who ftopped. Preached to them from
Mark xv. 16. Explained to them the gofpel, and
the circumftances which rendered it glad tidings to
every creature; fhewed that it was a difpenfation
wholly of grace, and that it was completely contradictory, both to fcripture and to fact, to reprefent
man as capable of doing any thing in order to render
himfelf acceptable to God. The pride of man indeed rejected this doctrine. He wifhed to recommend himfelf to God by his repentance, which
he confidered, and was taught to confider, as we
had heard from their minifter, as the equitable condition upon which God would be reconciled to
him. Endeavoured to fhew the inconfiftency of

this doctrine with the scripture-account of man's being naturally dead in trespasses and sins, and the vanity of all those hopes which were not founded upon the complete atonement of the Lord Jesus Christ. Told the people plainly, that what they had heard was not the gospel, and urged them to search the scriptures for themselves, mentioning at the same time, that our only motive in making these observations, was love to their immortal souls, whose final state we were convinced depended upon their belief or rejection of the gospel. As to their minister, we could have no ill will at him, but, on the contrary, sincerely prayed to God, that he might give him repentance to the acknowledgment of the truth.

On the same day, one of us went to Forfar, and preached at the cross. Began with three persons, who at first stood aloof. The congregation however increased to 100. Preached again in the evening to about 300, who were very attentive.

July 17. Preached at Kerrymuir, at seven o'clock in the morning, to about 400 people, many of whom had come from the country, having been hearers the evening before. Came to Forfar, where we preached in the street to a very attentive congregation. Heard with much regret that infidel principles had gained considerable ground in this place, and took occasion to warn them against Paine's Age of Reason, which we understood had been circulated amongst them.

Came to Brechin, about eight o'clock. Procured the town-hall, and sent intimation of sermon by the drum *. Preached to a crouded and attentive auditory.

---

* Intimations of this nature may, at first, hurt the feelings of some serious persons. But these emotions ought certainly to subfide, when such consider the vast importance of using every means to assemble careless sinners to hear the word of God, and the impossibility of our adopting any other mode equally effectual of giving general notice in our limited time.

July 18. After preaching in the morning at six o'clock, left Brechin, and came on to Montrose. Applied for the town-hall, but were refused on the ground that they had already enough of the gospel in Montrose. Understood, on our return, that the town-hall had been given to some of the people called Quakers, soon after we were there. We were kindly accommodated however with a meeting-house, where we preached in the evening and the next morning. We were sorry to learn, that many of the children in Montrose were unable to read, in consequence of going to the cotton-manufactory, at a very early period. They are greatly neglected too by their parents, and croud the streets on the Lord's day : a circumstance which seems to render the opinion expressed above of the abundance of the gospel somewhat doubtful. If true, its want of influence is deeply to be regretted.

July 19. Came forward through Bervie and Stonehaven, (at both of which places we preached twice), to Aberdeen, where we arrived the 21st.

The two last mentioned places appear to be in a most destitute situation with respect to the gospel. At Stonehaven particularly, we noticed the greatest indifference to the concerns of eternity that we had any where remarked. There are here two Episcopal chapels. The parish church is about the distance of a mile from the town.

July 22. Preached in the morning and evening in the College-court, Old Aberdeen. Intimated sermon by the drum for next evening, (Lord's day), in the College-close, New-Town.

Lord's-day, 23. Preached in the morning at Gilkomston and the Old Town. Went to one of the Magistrates, upon receiving information by the officer that they were displeased at our intimating sermon by the drum without their knowledge. He enquired whether we were preachers ? To this we anfwered in the affirmative. He expreffed a fear of our preaching fedition. We obferved to him, that the very circumftance of our giving fuch public intimation might fatisfy him that we had no intention of this kind. Told him that we alfo diftributed pamphlets, of which, if he was defirous of feeing them, we would fend him a fet. He faid this would be very proper, and accordingly a copy of each was fent him. Waited alfo upon the profeffors, who behaved with much civility. We now learned that we had done wrong in giving intimation of fermon in the College-clofe without confulting the profeffors, but this was owing entirely to mifinformation. In the evening one preached at Gilkomfton, (a place where the gofpel is greatly needed), another in a chapel in Aberdeen, and the third in the College-clofe to a great multitude, who almoft trod upon each other. The people behaved with the greateft decency and fhewed much attention. Took notice, at the beginning of our difcourfe at Gilkomfton, of the objections made by fome perfons againft the means employed for fending the gofpel abroad, from the confideration of the great ignorance that prevailed in fo many parts at home. A perfon after fermon told us, that a minifter in this neighbourhood had, a few weeks before, urged this very objection from the pulpit againft miffionary exertions, faying, That it was more neceffary to expend money in the inftruction of the ignorant, and of the youth at home. *Query*, Will this minifter's candour lead him now to retract his accufation, upon finding, that fince meafures have been taken for fending the gofpel abroad, no lefs anxiety has been fhewn to promote its influence among thofe who are as yet ftrangers to it at home?

Monday, 24. Preached in College-clofe, New-Town, at Gilkomfton, and Old-Town. Diftributed pamphlets, and then left Aberdeen. It muft give much pleafure to the friends of the truth to learn, that

within thefe five years, feveral faithful gofpel minifters have come to this city. The churches in confequence are much better attended, and we heard
with a mixture of joy and regret, that many people, efpecially in the neighbourhood, were difpofed
to attend the faithful publication of the gofpel, but
could get no accommodation in the places of worfhip
where it is preached. May the Lord foon fay to
that part of Zion, "Lengthen thy cords, and ftrength-
en thy ftakes." They have Sabbath-evening fchools
under the direction of the minifters and magiftrates;
but from the behaviour of the children upon difmiffion, which we were informed was very tumul-
tuous, there feems reafon to fear that they are attended with little benefit. We were forry to underftand that much of a party fpirit prevails amongft
the profeffors of religion in this city.

July 24. Came to Ellon. Preached in the evening and morning, and then came forward to Peter-
head. Sent immediate intimation of fermon, and
preached, about two hours after our arrival, from
the town-houfe ftairs, to a congregation of about
600 perfons. Preached in the morning before our
departure to about 350. The ftate of religion in
this place we underftand to be very low. Two or
three individuals came to us after fermon, expreffing
regret that we had faid nothing refpecting our return to them. An Antiburgher congregation has
been lately formed here, where we hope the gofpel
is preached.

July 26. Arrived at Fraferburgh in the evening.
Preached to one of the moft carelefs and unconcerned congregations that we had feen, or did fee, upon
the whole journey. Intimated fermon for next
morning at feven o'clock. Nobody appearing, we
delayed till nine. Went to the crofs, where we
preached. One man only was prefent when we
went out; in a little while, however, nearly 100 affembled, of whom not above one or two joined us in

finging. We found in moft places, that the people declined joining with us in the firft pfalm ; but generally a good many joined in the laft : in this place, however, they joined in neither. Of that town we apprehend it may juftly be faid, the fear of God is not in it. The truth is, in many parts of this country, the people enjoy no other means of religious inftrućtion, than barely hearing a fermon read to them upon the Lord's day, the purport of which often is, " If men do their beft, the Lord will accept them for Chrift's fake." This ferves at once to explain the total indifference that prevails throughout a great part of Scotland, not only to religion, but even to morals ; for the fountain being thus corrupted, it is not poffible that the ftreams can be pure.

Left Fraferburgh ; and being informed of a fmall town, named Rofehearty, a mile or two out of the road, we went thither and preached. When fending a lad through the village to warn the people, we mentioned as an inducement to their coming, that we would give them fome pamphlets. The landlady faid, fhe fuppofed thefe would be upon the ftate of the nation. When we told her that they refpećted the ftate of people's fouls, fhe feemed quite appalled, and inftantly left us. Came on through a hilly country to Banff, where we did not arrive till eleven o'clock at night.

July 28. After public intimation, one preached in the Relief meeting, Banff ; another at a village in the neighbourhood.

July 29. Preached in the morning at the Battery Green, and then feparated for the Lord's day ; one remained at Banff, another went to Portfoy, and the third to Cullen ; at all of which places, we preached on the Saturday evening, and thrice on the Lord's day, as well as once at the village adjoining Banff. As the parifh minifter did not preach at Banff, the one who remained there heard fermon in the Relief meeting. At Cullen, heard the minifter preach two difcourfes from 1 Cor. xv. 19. " If in this life only we have hope in Chrift, we are of all men moft miferable." The preacher faid, that men, in becoming Chriftians, certainly did renounce much pleafure in a prefent life ; but that the future would abundantly compenfate for what he feemed, from the tenor of his difcourfe, to reckon a very grievous facrifice. The comforts of Chriftianity in this fermon, were all confidered as future, and nothing but mifery its attendant in a prefent ftate. Preached immediately upon the difmiffion of the congregation. As the fermon which had been preached appeared to us, likely to excite averfion to Chriftianity, endeavoured, in oppofition to it, to ftate the doctrine of Scripture, that " godlinefs is profitable unto all things, having the promife of the life that now is, as well as of that which is to come," together with the declaration of Chrift, " My yoke is eafy, and my burden light."

Religion appears in all thefe places to be at a low ebb. There is at Banff, a Relief congregation, who are bleffed with a zealous and faithful minifter, and amongft whom are fome, we hope, who love the Lord Jefus Chrift. They form but a fmall proportion, however, of the inhabitants, of whom, as we were forry to learn, multitudes were in the habit of attending a band of mufic, which occupied the Battery Green, for a couple of hours every Lord's day evening. It is but juftice to fay, that on the evening we were there, the commanding-officer intermitted the parade, that the foldiers might have an opportunity of attending fermon.

A former minifter of this town publifhed a catechifm, in which he openly avowed Socinian principles, and his opinions, we underſtood, had made conſiderable progreſs among the people *. There is here a ſmall ſociety of Methodiſts, and a Roman Catholic congregation and prieſt. The Catholics here, as in ſome other parts of the North, are ſaid to be upon the increaſe, partly owing to the zeal of their clergy, and the want of zeal in others. There is alſo here an Epiſcopal meeting.

July 31. Met at Cullen, and after preaching and diſtributing pamphlets as uſual, went on to Fochabers, (a village in the neighbourhood at Gordon Caſtle). This place is notorious for its laxity of morals and indifference to religion. Of theſe we ſaw evident tokens, in the careleſſneſs and indifference of thoſe to whom we preached.

Auguſt 1. Arrived at Elgin. The magiſtrates and miniſters here prohibited the bell-man from giving intimation of ſermon; but though public notice was prevented, ſome friends of the truth were abundantly active, and at the appointed hour we had a congregation of about 600 perſons, to whom we

* The following are a few of the queſtions contained in this catechiſm. In Part III. "Q. Is it difficult to practiſe what God requires of us in the New Teſtament? A. Far from it, if we begin in time, and before we have contracted bad habits: But if we ſuffer any bad habits to grow upon us, it will be difficult then to do the contrary. Q. Which is the worſt of all bad habits? A. A habit of idleneſs. Q. Who was Jeſus Chriſt? A. The greateſt Prophet and the greateſt benefactor to mankind who ever appeared in the world. Q. What did Jeſus Chriſt do to take men out of their miſerable condition? A. To prove his divine miſſion, and engage the attention of mankind, he wrought many miracles; to ſuch as came to hear him he proclaimed the mercy of God for their paſt ſins, provided they would forſake them, and become his diſciples. Such as became his diſciples, he inſtructed in all the duties which God required of them, and to all who ſhould perſevere to the end in the performance of theſe duties, he promiſed eternal life. Q. In what reſpects was Jeſus Chriſt ſuperior to the prophets who came before him? A. In the perfection of his example, in the purity of his precepts, and in the importance of the motives by which he enforced them!" We heard, and we hope it may be true, that the Author of this catechiſm upon his death-bed deſired that all the copies ſhould be bought up and deſtroyed.

preached in the ftreet from the fteps of the church. Preached again in the morning. We found that the Socinian catechifm, formerly mentioned, had been introduced into the grammar-fchool of Elgin. At a public examination, however, upon one of the minifters of the prefbytery, who *preaches the gofpel*, remonftrating againft this innovation, (in which he was oppofed by the minifters of the town who were prefent), the Provoft ordered this new catechifm to be difcontinued, and the fhorter one of the Weftminfter affembly to be reftored. If, (as is affuredly the cafe), the belief of the doctrines of the gofpel be effentially neceffary to the formation of good principles, and if good principles be abfolutely neceffary, as will fcarcely be denied, to good conduct in the fubjects of any ftate ; we fcarcely think, that the inftilling of the doctrines of Socinianifm into the minds either of young or old can have any other effect than to loofen thofe bands of moral obligation by which fociety is linked together. They, and they only, are, as we apprehend, the true friends of government, who publifh thofe doctrines, which, not from the love or fear of man, but from that all powerful motive, the love of God, teach men to lead quiet and peaceable lives in all godlinefs and honefty, praying for kings and all in authority. There is in Elgin a chapel of eafe * and an Antiburgher congregation where the gofpel is preached. There are no Burghers beyond Aberdeen. There is a Sabbath evening-fchool, under the care of a pious young man, which it is hoped is doing good.

---

* The origin of this chapel is as follows. A very unpopular minifter being fettled at Elgin, the other minifter applied to the magiftrates for the ufe of an empty church to preach in, during the half of the day, in which, from the charge being collegiate, he was at liberty. This was granted. The people afterwards called a preacher, one and another has fucceeded, and in this way the gofpel ftill continues to be preached in Elgin. Neither baptifm, however, nor the Lord's fupper, are allowed to be difpenfed in that Chapel.

Auguſt 2. Came to Forres, and preached at the croſs to about 800 people. Saw a woman in much diſtreſs of mind, but evidently under the Lord's teaching. Came to Auldearn, (where we underſtood the goſpel had been greatly needed for 50 years paſt), and preached. Were happy to hear, that the goſpel was now preached in an Antiburgher congregation in the pariſh.

Auguſt 3. Came to Nairn, and preached in the evening and next morning to about 600 people, each time in the ſtreet. Met with a moſt affectionate reception here from ſome friends of the goſpel, of the Antiburgher congregation. The intereſts of Chriſt's kingdom ſeem to flouriſh in this congregation. They have a monthly meeting, where Chriſtians of different denominations join in prayer for the ſucceſs of the goſpel, and for a bleſſing upon thoſe exertions which are making by the different Miſſionary Societies. They have alſo a Sabbathevening ſchool under the care of ſome of their members.

Auguſt 4. Went to Fort George in the hope of being allowed to preach to the ſoldiers. Upon application being made to the Governor, he declined granting us liberty, alleging that he never heard of ſermon in any fort on a week day. He ſaid we might preach on the Sabbath. Accordingly one remained and preached on that day in the fort, and twice each day on Saturday and the Lord's day at Campbelltown, (a village adjoining the fort), where we had alſo preached on Friday evening, the 4th inſt.

Auguſt 5. Two went forward to Inverneſs. On our way thither, met numbers of people returning from hearing ſermon, (being the Saturday previous to the ſacrament), who had come from places ten, twelve and fifteen miles diſtant, to hear ſome faithful miniſters, who aſſiſt on thoſe occaſions.

Lord's day, August 6. Preached in the morning at eight o'clock, on a hill adjoining the town; again in the ftreet at one, and at four and feven o'clock in the evening, to very large congregations, from 1500 to 2000 perfons.

Auguft 7. Preached morning and evening in the ftreet to very great multitudes. Had a meeting with fome friends, who formed themfelves into a Society for erecting Sabbath-evening fchools. This Society has fince eftablifhed three fchools in Invernefs, all of which are well attended.

Having heard while at Elgin, that a fair was foon to be held at Kirkwall, at which there were ufually great numbers of people from the different Ifles of Orkney; and having alfo heard of the deplorable ftate of many of thofe iflands from the want of religious inftruction, we refolved that two of us fhould embrace the opportunity of going thither with the merchants from Elgin, and then return through Caithnefs, Sutherland and Rofsfhires to Invernefs, in which place and neighbourhood we thought it moft advifeable for one to ftay and labour, till the other two fhould return. Accordingly, after preaching on Tuefday morning to about 500 people, who ftood all the time though it rained, we left Invernefs on our return to Elgin. Came to Nairn, where we preached in the evening to about 700 perfons from the town-houfe ftairs. Our friends told us, they had had a miffionary prayer-meeting the evening before. This meeting, as has been mentioned, is held monthly. The members without refpect of party engage in prayer, and offer obfervations upon the prefent appearances of God in behalf of the heathen, with the probable effects of thefe upon the ftate of religion at home. Were thankful to learn, that the object of our journey had been the means of exciting their zeal, and that, when it was the fubject of converfa-

E

tion at their meetings, they had enjoyed tokens of the divine prefence.

Auguft 9. Preached at Nairn to about 750, at Auldearn to 300, and at Forres to 450, and then came on to Elgin, where we arrived late in the evening.

Auguft 10. Preached in the ftreet to about 700 in the morning at nine o'clock, and to about 1000 in the evening. The audiences, as in every place between this and Invernefs, were very attentive.

Auguft 11. Left Elgin and came to Brughhead, where a good many of our friends from Elgin, and the people of the village affembled, to whom we preached. We then embarked for Kirkwall. Several of our brethren accompanied us to the boat, and bade us farewell, moft affectionately commending us to the grace and care of the Lord Jefus. Sailed with a fair wind. It fell calm in the afternoon, and the wind feemed likely to become foul, but by the kindnefs of providence a fair and brifk gale fprung up, which brought us fafely into Scalpa Bay, about a mile from Kirkwall, by eight o'clock next morning. The merchants who freighted the boat, and the failors in general, behaved to us with much kindnefs ; and, as we prefumed, from refpect to us, made a law, that whoever fhould fwear an oath fhould receive corporal punifhment, which they occafionally carried into execution. Preached in the boat on the Friday evening. They liftened with much attention, and frequently attended afterwards, during our ftay at Kirkwall.

Auguft 12. Arrived at Kirkwall. Were providentially directed to a friend of the truth, who received us with much kindnefs. Intimated fermon by the bell at half paft fix in the evening, in the Palace-clofe, where we preached to a congregation of about 800 perfons. This is a fquare, formed by a large and ancient edifice, on the fouth, fuppofed to have been the palace of fome of the Norwegian kings, and on the north by another, termed the Bifhop's palace. On the eaft is the church of St Magnus, and on the weft it is bounded by a wall. It is capable probably of containing ten or twelve thoufand perfons. Having heard that there had been only two or three fermons preached in the ifland of Shappinfhay, a few miles diftant from Kirkwall, from the time of the laft General Affembly that their minifter had left them, we refolved that one of us fhould fpend the Lord's day in that ifland, while the other remained in Kirkwall. The minifter of Shappinfhay was at this time detained in Edinburgh, as an evidence in a trial; but it is well known to be the practice of minifters from that country, to take a confiderable vacation at the time of the General Affembly.

Before proceeding further in the account of our labours, we fhall here offer a few remarks on the former and prefent religious ftate of Orkney. The iflands of Orkney, according to our information, which is rendered ftrongly credible by what we actually witneffed, have been, for a period beyond the memory of any man living, (excepting in one or two folitary inftances), as much in need of the true gofpel of Jefus Chrift, fo far as refpects the preaching of it, as any of the iflands of the Pacific Ocean. Many of the parifhes comprehend two or three different iflands. In each of thefe the minifter fhould preach occafionally; but owing to the want of churches, or rather to the churches being in want of repair, as well as to the occafional trouble and difficulty of croffing the friths which interfect thefe iflands, to fay nothing of want of zeal, many of the people fee their paftor but feldom in the courfe of the year. It is a fact, that in fome cafes where there are two iflands in a parifh, or two parifhes annexed in one ifland, and a church in repair

E 2

only in one of them, the minifter preaches in it the
one Sabbath, but the next, when it falls to the turn of
the other ifland or parifh, he neither preaches there,
nor in his other church, though it may adjoin his
manfe.

It can give no furprife to thofe who know the
gofpel, and are acquainted with that enmity and oppofition which the human mind naturally bears to
its humiliating doctrines, to learn that the fermons
of fuch paftors do not contain glad tidings to perifhing finners. At the fame time, one would think
that the moft inconfiderate could fcarcely fail to be
ftruck with the ftrange inconfiftency of teaching o-
thers that they will be faved by a diligent difcharge
of the duties of their ftation, while they themfelves
fo openly neglect their own. The manners and
conduct of the people, as in every other place, are
corrupted in a due proportion to their ignorance of
the gofpel, and to no part in Orkney, as we learn,
did this remark more juftly apply, than it did about
five or fix years ago to Kirkwall, where, excepting
two or three individuals, the great body of the
people were utter ftrangers to the doctrine of juftification by faith in the death and refurrection of
Chrift, without works. It pleafed God, however,
in the riches of his grace, to look down with ten-
der compaffion upon the deplorable fituation of this
place, and to fend them help out of his holy heaven.
A native of Orkney, who had been apprentice to a
pious tradefmen in Kirkwall, went to Newcaftle,
where he attended with profit the miniftry of Mr
Graham, the Antiburgher. He returned to Kirkwall, and having experienced the benefit of religious
fociety in the fouth, upon finding another perfon of
views fimilar to his own, he propofed a weekly meeting
for prayer and religious fellowfhip. This was immediately formed. One and another, whofe minds
it pleafed God, by means of converfation or read-

ing books which were put into their hands, to bring
under impreffions of the infinite worth of their immortal fouls, were added to their little meeting.
Their numbers continued from time to time to increafe. Thefe perfons now began ferioufly to feel
their ftate of bondage with regard to religious privileges. They found it was a yoke which they
were not able to bear, and therefore determined,
looking up to God for his countenance, to open a
fubfcription for erecting a place of worfhip, where they
might enjoy the bleffing of the preaching of the gofpel. Their means were indeed but very flender, and
appeared little likely to accomplifh the end, efpecially
in the view of that oppofition, with which they knew
they muft contend. But He, whofe glory it is to
chufe the weak things of this world to confound
the mighty, appeared moft eminently in their behalf, and they were enabled both to begin and to
finifh a houfe for the worfhip of God. They then
applied to the Antiburgher Synod for a minifter to
preach to them. A minifter was accordingly fent,
and others fucceffively fince that time, all of whofe
labours appear to have been remarkably bleffed.
Many who were living altogether carelefs of divine
things, fince the gofpel was preached in the New
Church, as it is called, have been brought under
ferious concern, and give good evidence, by their
conduct, that they are paffed from death unto life ;
and fome who were avowed enemies have become
the friends of the caufe. The Lord appears evidently to have been preparing a people in this place
for himfelf ; and it is remarked, that fince the time
that this uncommon concern hath been excited, a
very confiderable external reformation has taken
place, even amongft thofe who do not appear to be
under the influence of the truth. That the Lord's
arm hath been made bare in behalf of thefe deftitute
ifles, in no common way, will appear from the fact,

·that two hundred perfons were admitted to the
Lord's fupper, upon the firft celebration of that ordinance in July laft, after a ftrict and individual examination, in which the minifters enjoyed, as we are
informed, much fatisfaction. Several alfo were kept
back, of whom good hopes are entertained. When
the circumftance juft ftated is contrafted with the
fituation of Kirkwall but four or five years fince, the
friends of Chrift may well exclaim with joy and gra-
titude, " What hath God wrought !" " The wildernefs hath truly rejoiced ; it hath bloffomed as the rofe.
The Lord's arm is not yet fhortened that it cannot
fave, neither is his ear heavy that it cannot hear.''

This new-church met at firft with confiderable
oppofition. Much influence was ufed to deter fuch as
were in dependent circumftances from attending it.
In confequence, however, of a threatning from fome
of the members to lay before the public an account
of the proceedings of their moft active opponents,
they became much lefs violent, and now the congregation comparatively enjoys peace.

Lord's day, 13*th Auguft*. Preached in the morning to between 1200 or 1300 perfons. Went to the
eftablifhed church and heard fermon by a neighbouring minifter from Job xxviii. 28. " Behold the
fear of the Lord, that is wifdom." The whole of
the fear of the Lord and of religion he comprehended
in the difcharge of the focial duties, of which the
chief that he infifted upon, was honefty in their deal-
ings with each other. This was the only way, he
faid, by which man could recommend himfelf to the
favour of God. The name of the Lord Jefus Chrift
was not once mentioned in the whole of the fermon.
Indeed, upon the plan of it, there was no need of
his interpofition.——Had the happinefs to hear the
gofpel preached in the afternoon in the Antiburgher
meeting. The houfe is unfortunately too fmall : it
cannot accommodate all the hearers. It may hold

about 700 people. In the evening preached to about 3000 hearers, from Pilate's queſtion, John xviii. 38. " What is truth?" Endeavoured, at conſiderable length, to point out the inconſiſtency of what had been preached in the forenoon, with the truth as it is in Jeſus Chriſt. Referred to the penances of the Church of Rome, and obſerved that on account of adding theſe to the atonement of Chriſt, as the foundation of hope, it had been denounced by the Church of Scotland, as *the mother of abominations*. Took notice that every miniſter acknowledged this, when he ſigned the confeſſion of faith, and then aſked, whether teaching men to truſt in their own honeſty, without regard to Chriſt at all, was not equally, if not more groſs, than any of the doćtrines of the Romiſh church? It was truly affećting to remark the concern of thoſe who loved the Lord Jeſus Chriſt, and who no doubt recollećted the huſks upon which they had formerly fed, on hearing that his name had not been mentioned, in a ſermon addreſſed to periſhing men. They gave a mournful ſhriek, ſuch as we ſhould conceive perſons to give upon ſeeing a fellow-creature receive the ſtroke of death.

Agreeably to our determination, one of us went to Shappinſhay, (a boat being ſent by the people). Preached twice by the ſea-ſide to about 500 people, who were very attentive. After ſermon went to ſee an old man, ninety-two years of age, confined to bed. Found him hardly able to ſpeak, but quite ſenſible. Aſked him, if he knew what was to become of him after death? He ſaid he was very ignorant, could not read, but had ſometimes prayed to God. On being aſked, whether he knew any thing of Chriſt? he acknowledged his entire ignorance. Preached the goſpel to him, declaring that now the Lord was waiting to be gracious; and that if he believed what the word of God teſtified of his guilt and miſery, and of the perſon and work of Chriſt, whoſe divine charaćter we particularly inſiſted upon, he fhould be faved. He feemed much affected, and grafped the fpeaker eagerly by the hand. He cried to God for the pardon of his fins ; and being inform- ed that his prayers could only be heard through Jefus Chrift, who came to fave the very chief of fin- ners,. he called upon the Saviour for mercy, and repeatedly exclaimed, *I believe, I believe.* This re- called ftrongly to our mind the cafe of the blind man, who, as foon as he knew the Son of God, worfhip- ped him. Vifited alfo a woman, who had been long ill, and whofe affliction appeared to have been great- ly bleffed to her. She expreffed much thankfulnefs for it, and was defirous, if it were the will of God, to depart and to be with Chrift. Returned to Kirk- wall in the evening.

Auguft 14.The fair began this day.. Preached in the Palace-clofe in the morning to about 1200, and in the evening to about 2300 hearers. Many of the people appeared much affected, and in tears.

Auguft 15. Went to Stromnefs.. Preached to a- bout 500 perfons, and next day to much the fame number. Religion is very low in this town. We met with one friend of the truth, who told us, that he could not find another perfon in the town to join with him in a meeting for Chriftian conference and pray- er. Urged him ftrongly to fet on foot a Sabbath- evening fchool, to which he feemed well inclined. Went to Hoy, and faw Mr H——— the minifter, lately fettled here. He appeared to us to be truly defirous of promoting the fpiritual interefts of his people. We were happy to find that in the adjoin- ing ifland, a part of his charge, where the church is in ruins, he had been preaching to the people in the open air. The conduct of Mrs H——— alfo de- ferves peculiar notice and commendation. On the Lord's day evenings, fhe employs herfelf in teach- ing a number of children both to read the word of God, and to underftand its leading and important. doctrines. May the Lord crown fo exemplary a la--

bour of love with his own rich and effectual bleffing !
Returned to Kirkwall, and preached in the evening
to nearly 2000 people. Received preffing invita-
tions to vifit different places.

Auguft 17. Preached in the morning to about
2000, and in the evening to about 4000 perfons.
A great many lovers of the truth called upon us
this day, expreffing, as others formerly, much intereft in the object of our labours. A perfon from
Egglefay, (one of the iflands), called upon us. He
wifhed much that we fhould reprefent the defolate
fituation of that ifland. It is united with that of
Roufay, and the minifter having been laid up by
palfy for fix years, in all this time they had only had
three fermons. He mentioned, that the people were
intending to fend a petition to the General Affembly.

Auguft 18. Preached in the morning to upwards
of 3000, and in the evening to upwards of 4000
perfons, according to our eftimation, and that of o-
thers. Went this day to Shappinfhay, to vifit the
old man formerly mentioned. Found him unable
to fpeak, but fenfible. He knew us immediately,
and defired by figns to be lifted up in the bed.
He was fupported while we fpoke to him, was much
affected, and difcovered that he underftood what
was faid to him. Upon afking him, whether he
wifhed us to pray, he fhewed his defire, as far as
poffible, by attempting to fpeak. His wife faid,
that he had wept much after our leaving him the
former day. She had occafionally read to him parts
of the fcriptures. He died on the next Lord's
day. Saw another fick man ; he feemed to have
fome knowledge, but did not appear to be much affected with the truth. Saw alfo the woman formerly mentioned, who was in much pain, but expreffed an unfhaken confidence in the Lord Jefus.
Preached afterwards to about 60 people, and then
returned to Kirkwall.

August 19. Preached in the morning and evening to about the fame numbers as formerly.

We have here much reafon to remark the goodnefs of God in difpofing the people, the whole time the fair lafted, to continue with regularity, in their attendance. The fair was in a meafure emptied every evening. May he whofe blefling alone giveth the increafe, be pleafed gracioufly to water the feed which hath been fown with the dew of heaven, caufing it to take root downward, and to bring forth fruit upward, to the praife of the glory of his own rich and fovereign grace!

The fame day one of us went to Orfer (about five miles from Kirkwall), and preached to about 200, who were very attentive, and fome of them much affected. The minifter of this place had been at Edinburgh for feveral months, and had fent no perfon to officiate in his place.

Lord's day, 20*th August.* Preached in the morning, again at one o'clock, and at four and fix in the evening. The hearers of the two laft fermons were fuppofed to be near 6000. Heard fermon by a neighbouring minifter in the Eftablifhed Church. He preached from Pfal. xcvii. 11. " Light is fown for the righteous." He fuppofed men to be firft righteous, and then fomehow enjoying benefits by Chrift. It was who ly upon the fyftem of works. He faid, that the great principles of morality, juftice, love, &c. were naturally implanted in our hearts, but clouded with prejudice. He did not mention the corruption of human nature. Took particular notice of it in one of our fermons, and fhewed its inconfiftency with the fcriptures.

21*st August.* Preached in the morning to about 900, and in the evening to about 1700, many of the people having now left the fair. One of us went to Rendal, and preached to about 300 perfons.

Rendal and Eva form one parish. At the latter place, owing to the ruinous state of the church, there has been no sermon for eight or nine years, and by no means regularly at the other; at the utmost, never oftener than the alternate Sabbath, as formerly noticed. Afterwards went to the island of Egglefay and preached. This island, with that of Roufay, are united in one parish. The minister, as has been mentioned, had been laid entirely aside, by a stroke of the palfy, for the last six or feven years, and had never provided a helper. The people meet in church, and sermons are read to them by the proprietor of the island, when at home. On speaking to them of their situation, they appeared much affected.

August 22. Preached in the morning to about 1500, and in the evening to about 2000. One went to Tankernefs, and preached to about 500 people. Saw a perfon ill of a fever this evening, a little way out of Kirkwall. Had much fatisfaction in the account which he gave of his views both of his own character and that of the Saviour. He was a hearer in the New Church. Vifited feveral other fick people.

August 23. Left Kirkwall on a tour through the northern ifles. We feparated, having each of us a companion: one of us took the clufter of ifles to the right, the other that to the left.

The former embarked for Eday, but were obliged to land in Shappinfhay, and to wait near two hours for the tide. Went to a houfe, expounded the fcriptures, and prayed. Got to Eday at about one o'clock. Gave intimation of fermon. Vifited fome fick people very ignorant. Preached to about 300. Croffed to Sanday. Had fome trouble in getting a lodging. By the kindnefs of providence were at length well accommodated. Converfed a confiderable time with the mafter of the houfe, who

had been long ill, and was very ignorant. Sent intimation of fermon through the ifland.

Thurfday, Auguft 24. Preached to about 750
perfons. Intimated fermon at the other end of the
ifland. Went thither and preached to much the
fame number. Croffed the ferry to North Ronaldfhay in forty-five minutes, an uncommonly quick
paffage; arrived about eight o'clock. Saw a fick
man, brother to our companion, who appeared to
be dying in the faith. They had had five fermons
in this ifland fince laft year. There is no fchool in
the ifland. Sent a propofal to the proprietor to erect
a fchool, provided he would give land for a houfe
and a cow's grafs; but this we fince find, he has re-
fufed.

Auguft 25. Preached to about 350 people, and
re-croffed the frith to Sanday. Vifited fome fick
people, all very ignorant. Upon afking one woman
the foundation of her hope, fhe faid, fhe had not
been fuch a finner as to be afraid. Croffed to Stronfay about ten o'clock at night, where we arrived.

Auguft 26. Saw a fick man, who appeared to be
a Chriftian. Thus, one and another of the fheep of
Chrift are occafionally found in places where they
are leaft-expected. Preached to nearly 800 people.
Saw fome Chriftian women. Eight had formed themfelves into a fellowfhip-meeting, four of whom accompanied us about four miles to the fea-fide. Left
Stronfay, arrived at Shappinfhay, walked acrofs it;
and, by the good providence of God, arrived at Kirkwall between eleven and twelve o'clock.

Lord's day, Auguft 27. Preached in the evening
in the Palace-clofe to about 2500. Heard the Antiburgher minifter.

Monday, Auguft 28. Preached at nine o'clock
to about 2000, and then went and preached at Deernefs, to about 800 people; and afterwards at Tankernefs on the way back. Thefe two places are

united in one parish; but as there is no church at
Deernefs, the minifter never preaches there.

Our brother returned this afternoon from his expedition to the other iflands.

Here follows his journal.

Auguft 23. Left Kirkwall; and, after a tedious
paffage of fix hours, arrived at Roufay. Sent intimation of fermon to Egglefhay, the adjoining ifland,
for the afternoon; the people being more readily
collected there than at Roufay. Sent intimation alfo
through Roufay for fermon there next morning.
Went over to Egglefhay, accompanied by fome of
the people of Roufay, and preached to about 200 perfons. Returned to Roufay, and lodged by invitation
from Mrs L——, (from whom we received much
eivility), at the houfe of Mr L——, the minifter
formerly mentioned as being ill of the palfy. He
was at the point of death when we came there, and
died the fame night.

Auguft 24. Preached at Roufay in the morning
to upwards of 300 people. When fpeaking to them
of their fituation, in having been fo long without the
preaching of the gofpel, the whole congregation
feemed deeply affected. Some perfons wept aloud
during the greater part of the fermon. We told
them that we did not confider their fituation as
having been more deftitute than that of many other
parts in Orkney. On the contrary, if they had been
led by this means more ferioufly to attend to the
fcriptures, their want of ordinances might have proved to them a great blefling. Left Roufay, and came
to Weftray. Sent intimation of fermon for next
morning through the ifland. Walked acrofs it, and
took a boat to Papay Weftray; a fmall adjoining
ifland, where we preached the fame evening to about
feventy perfons, and then returned to Weftray, to
lodge all night.

Auguft 25. A number of people, about 300,
came from the different quarters of the ifland, al-

though it rained all the morning. We had no fhelter, but the rain went off moſt providentially when we began to preach. Intimated fermon for the afternoon on the other fide of the ifland. Went to fee a fick man. He was grofsly ignorant of the gofpel, and yet trufting, as he faid, to the mercy of God. Attempted to explain the gofpel to him, and prayed. On our way to the other fide of the ifland, were entreated to vifit a fick man, upwards of ninety years of age. He knew nothing of Jefus Chriſt, and was fo deaf that we were incapable of fpeaking to him at any length, or of making him underſtand what was faid. Had been confined to bed two years; but his wife told us was feldom or never vifited by any perfon. Preached to about 500 people. Went afterwards to fee a farmer, in circumſtances of the greateſt external fuffering. He had been for a long time grievoufly afflicted with a cancer in his nofe, which had, in a great meafure, deſtroyed the organs of fpeech. He fpoke with much difficulty. Did not feem to have diſtinct views of the gofpel, but appeared fo deeply affected when we fpoke to him of the fufferings of God in our nature, as led us ſtrongly to hope that his affliction had been fanctified to him. He had been much employed, we were informed, during his illnefs, in the perufal of the fcriptures.

Auguſt 26. Left Weſtray, and came to Fairy, a fmall ifland containing about fifty perfons. There is no preaching here at any time. If the people are inclined to hear, they muſt go to a neighbouring ifland which is occafionally vifited. Preached to about thirty perfons. Two women appeared much affected. Converfed with fome perfons, ignorant of the gofpel as heathens, one of whom was much advanced in life. How true is Solomon's declaration, " Where there is no vifion, the people perifh." Left Fairy, and came to Egglefhay. Sent immediate intimation of fermon. Preached to about 200 perfons in the expectation of leaving them immediately. It began to rain, and the wind being contrary, we were obliged, but by no means unwillingly, to remain at Egglefhay for the Lord's day.

Lord's day, August 27. Gave intimation of fermon to the Roufay people by lighting fires. Preached at eleven o'clock, and again at four o'clock, to upwards of 400 perfons. Came to Roufay in the evening, and gave an exhortation to feveral perfons affembled for Mr L——'s funeral.

Monday, August 28. Left Roufay, and arrived at Kirkwall about two o'clock. Preached our laft fermon in the Palace-clofe, to about 2000 perfons. The people appeared much affected at our leaving them. A young woman was brought to us after fermon, whofe heart it had pleafed God deeply to pierce with the arrows of conviction. She had been for fome time under ferious concern of mind, and had been attending the means of grace. She expreffed a ftrong defire of being enabled to lay hold on Chrift by faith. We told her that the faith by which ungodly finners were juftified, did not confift in vigorous exertions of the mind, but in a perfuafion of the truth revealed in the fcriptures concerning the character and work of Chrift. She faid this was comfortable ; fhe hoped fhe believed the word of God.

We may here alfo mention that we were attended at family-prayer by as many as the room could contain, during the whole of our ftay in Kirkwall.

August 29. Left Kirkwall, accompanied by many of our dear brethren as far as Holm, where we preached to 1100 perfons, who had affembled in confequence of previous intimation. The minifter whofe fermon we had occafion to notice from Job xxviii. 28. was about to be tranflated to this parifh. We learned that only feven perfons had figned his call.

Took leave of our dear Chriftian friends, and croffed over to Burra, a fmall ifland, where one ftaid and preached to about 100, while the other went forward to South Ronaldfhay, and preached to about forty.

Auguft 30. Preached at the north fide of South Ronaldfhay to about 350 people, and at the Ferry to about 150. We here parted with our two friends who had accompanied us in our expedition through the ifles. One of them, who had been employed for fome time on the Sabbath in catechifing children, and whofe endeavours God had been pleafed in fome meafure to countenance, expreffed a ftrong defire of being more extenfively employed in the work. After examining him refpecting his knowledge, and parti-cularly enquiring into his character, it appeared to us that he might be very ufeful in vifiting the iflands as a catechift. He is accordingly now engaged in that work.

We cannot here pafs by a fact related to us by one of the friends juft mentioned, as it ferves ftrong-ly to illuftrate the power of divine grace, and the variety of ways in which the Lord leads men to the knowledge of the truth. While our friend was en-gaged one morning with his family in praifing God, a perfon paffed his houfe, and obferved his cow ftanding in a place where it had been left for the time without food. This led him to contraft their conduct with his own. Thefe people, thought he, are more concerned about their fouls than about their cattle, while I am wholly engroffed with my worldly intereft. A train of reflections fucceed-ed, and he is now a member of the New Church. He told our friend fome time ago, that the cir-cumftance juft related was that which firft led him to think of his ftate before God.

Croffed the Pentland frith in about two hours, being favoured with moderate weather. It becomes us here to remark the goodnefs of God to us in this refpect, both in croffing the different friths, and du-

ring the whole of our ſtay in Kirkwall, having never once been incommoded, while preaching, with
rain, although ſometimes the clouds had a lowering
aſpect. Walked two miles from the place of land-
ing to Hoonah, to the great inconvenience of one of
us, who bruiſed his leg in coming from Eggleſhay,
a circumſtance which, though apparently trivial at
firſt, yet afterwards materially altered the plan of
our journey, detaining us ſix weeks in the county
of Caithneſs, inſtead of a fortnight, as we had at firſt
intended.

31ſt *Auguſt*. Arrived at Thurſo. Could procure no lodging at the inn, on account of a fair, to
begin the following day. Providentially, however,
a gentleman, to whom we had letters, moſt kindly
offered us accommodation at his houſe, and we abode
there during the whole of our ſtay in Thurſo. Our
brother who met with the accident mentioned above,
was confined here in the houſe, for upwards of four
weeks. But even in this ſituation, from the earneſt
deſire of many to hear the word of God, he was not
wholly ſhut up from uſefulneſs, having opportunity
every evening of ſpeaking to a congregation of from
50 to 60 and ſometimes 100. They continued to
attend during the whole of our ſtay.—Intimated ſermon by the bell, and preached in the yard of the Antiburgher meeting-houſe, to about 300 perſons, who
ſeemed rather unconcerned.

September 1. Preached in the morning to about
200, and in the evening to about 500 people. They
ſeemed more attentive than the former congregations.

September 2. Preached in the Antiburgher meeting-houſe with which our brethren of that congregation readily accommodated us, as it rained. There
might to be about 800 perſons, within and without.
In the evening, preached in a large yard, where we
continued to meet when fair, to about 1500 hearers.

Lord's day, 3. Preached at half paft 9 o'clock to about 1700 people. It began to rain, but no perfon moved. Went to church, and heard the minifter of a neighbouring parifh preach from Gal. vi. 4. " But let every man prove his own work, and then fhall be have rejoicing in himfelf alone, and not in another." He recommended to his hearers to examine their conduct and the motives of it, laying afide entirely every degree of prejudice, and if they found themfelves holy, they would then have caufe of rejoicing, and enjoy the peace of God in their confciences. The law of God, he faid, only required fincere and not perfect obedience, and he cautioned men againft trufting in the blood of Chrift alone for acceptance with God. His peace-fpeaking blood was for the holy and the good ! Preached in the evening to about 3000 people, and bore teftimony againft the doctrine which had been preached in the forenoon, as being directly fubverfive of the gofpel.

Monday, Tuefday, and Wednefday, Sept. 4, 5, 6. Preached morning and evening each day ; congregations of 700 and 800 to 1000, and very attentive.

Thurfday, 7. Went to Reifter in the parifh of Dunnet, and preached to about 300 people. Afterwards went to Cleoch, parifh of Bower, and preached to about 400. The laft congregation was very attentive. It rained during the whole of the fermon, but none of the people moved, except one woman.

Friday and Saturday, 8. and 9. Preached at Thurfo morning and evening to from 700 to 800 people each time.

Lord's day, 10th *Sept.* Preached at 10 o'clock to from 2000 to 3000 people, many of whom had come from the country. Preached again at two o'clock to upwards of 3000 perfons from 2d Epiftle of John, verfes 10. and 11. " If there come any unto you and bring not this doctrine, receive him not

into your houfe, neither bid him God fpeed, for he
that biddeth him God fpeed is partaker of his evil
deeds." We reckoned this fubject peculiarly neceffary, as we found that feveral perfons, whofe eyes
the Lord had opened to difcern the truth, continued
ftill to attend the miniftry of falfe teachers, which
appeared to us a direct violation of the pofitive precept contained in the words of the apoftle : a cuftom
we fear too prevalent elfewhere. In the evening
preached to much the fame number as in the morning. Made a collection to defray the expences of
accomodation for the mafter of the fchool in this
place, belonging to the Society for propagating
Chriftian knowledge in Scotland, the managers
having difcontinued a ball, which they held for that
purpofe, at this feafon. The collection we were
happy to find exceeded what was ufually collected
at the ball.

Monday, 11. Went, according to invitation, to
the parifh of Olrig, and preached to about 300. Afterwards went to Quarry-crook, in the parifh of Hal-
kirk, and preached to upwards of 600. Saw a
young woman, who had been confined to bed for
14 years, and whofe affliction appeared to have been
fanctified.

Tuefday, 12. Went to Shempfter in the parifh of
Reay. Preached to from 200 to 300 people in a
large barn. The inclemency of the weather, from
conftant rain and the fwelling of a river, prevented
many people from coming to the meeting, who
would otherwife have attended.

Wednefday, 13. Preached in the meeting-houfe to
about 600 perfons. Being ftill detained at Thurfo,
we thought it advifeable that one fhould go to the
ifland of Walls in Orkney, to which we had received an invitation while at Kirkwall. Accordingly he hired a boat, and left Thurfo about one
o'clock ; arrived in Walls at four o'clock, after a

very favourable paſſage. Sent intimation of ſermon through the iſland for next day at ten o'clock.
Lodged with a perſon who had invited us to this iſland.

Thurſday, 14. The people were late in aſſembling,
many of them having a ferry to croſs. Preached
at twelve o'clock to above 200 people. After ſermon went to Flota, (a neighbouring iſland), and
preached to about 40 people. Viſited an old
woman confined to bed. She was groſsly ignorant, and hoped for future happineſs, as ſhe ſaid,
ſhe had done nothing bad in this world, excepting
once that ſhe had had an illegitimate child. Returned to Walls, and viſited ſome ſick perſons. They
were all very ignorant, but one of them, who had
been long lame, appeared much affected in hearing
the goſpel.

Friday, 15. In the morning, viſited an old woman, who ſaid ſhe was within one year of 100.
She ſeemed altogether ignorant of the goſpel, but
without any apprehenſions of the danger of her
ſtate. Saw a ſick man alſo very ignorant. Preached at 12 o'clock to nearly 200 people, many of
whom were much affected ; as indeed they were
in every iſland of Orkney where we preached. Several of the Flota people were preſent, but none
from another ſmall adjoining iſland, named Fairy,
where are ſix or eight families, to whom intimation had been ſent. Several people from the neighbourhood were preſent at family-worſhip.

Saturday, 16. Re-croſſed the Pentland Frith, and
by the divine goodneſs arrived at Thurſo between
ſix and ſeven in the evening.

Lord's day, 17. Preached in the morning to about
1500 people. Heard afterwards the pariſh miniſter
preach from Titus iii. 8. "Theſe things I will that
thou affirm conſtantly, that they who have believed
in God, might be careful to maintain good works.

Thefe things are good and profitable unto men." He
feemed much afraid of people abufing the doctrines
of grace, and therefore told them that though they
were to be juftified freely by grace, yet that afterwards
they muft be juftified partly by faith and partly by
works. The Jewish teachers he faid defpifed works,
and that all the apoftles, and efpecially Paul, wrote
aguinft fuch doctrine. People, he added, were
ready to build all their hopes upon Chrift; and
therefore it was neceffary that it fhould, on all
occafions, be affirmed, that they who had believed fhould be careful to maintain good works,
in order to entitle them to falvation. He then
gave intimation that there would be no fermon in
the afternoon during the remainder of the feafon.
It is the regular practice, it feems, through this
part of the country, as it is indeed in other places
farther fouth, to have only one difcourfe of half an
hour's length in the day during nearly nine months
of the year. This was probably an advantage in
Thurfo, as it led many people in the afternoon to
hear a godly man, the Antiburgher minifter, who
was long fettled there, but died in June laft.

Preached in the evening to about 3000 perfons,
from Eph. ii. 8, 10. " For by grace are ye faved,
through faith, and that not of yourfelves, it is the
gift of God. Not of works left any man fhould
boaft," &c. Took particular notice of the fermon that had been preached. Obferved that good
works could not be too much infifted upon, if
fpoken of as an effect of faith, but that thofe
who ftated them as the ground of a finner's acceptance and juftification, rendered Chrift of none effect,
like the judaizing teachers, who taught men that,
except they were circumcifed, they could not be faved. To thofe who imbibed this doctrine, the apoftle folemnly teftified, that Chrift fhould profit them
nothing, Gal. v. 2. The fpeaker then told them,

that he had found it to be his duty, however unpleasant, to bear testimony against the doctrine which he had heard from their minister, but that though he might be detained another Sabbath in Thurso, he would not again attend their church.

Monday, 18. Preached in the morning to about 600 people, and in the evening to about 800.

Tuesday, 19. After preaching in the morning, went to Thurdistaff in the parish of Olrig, and preached to about 600 people.

Wednesday, 20. Went to Mey in the parish of Cannisbay, and preached to about 200 people. They were very careless and inattentive. Went afterwards to Ratter in the parish of Dunnet, and preached to about 120 persons. Returned to Thurso.

Thursday, 21. and *Friday*, 22. Preached to congregations, from 500 to 700 and 800, morning and evening.

Saturday, 23. Preached in the meeting-house, morning and evening, the rain preventing our meeting in the yard, as usual.

Lord's day, 24. The weather being uncommonly fine, preached in the yard to about 3000 people in the morning.

As one of us who had been hitherto confined appeared likely to be able to get out in the course of a few days ; we thought it adviseable that the other, upon whom the whole of the public labour had devolved, should spend the remaining part of the time we were to stay in Caithness, in the town of Wick and its neighbourhood. In the view, therefore, of leaving Thurso on the next day, he preached in the evening a farewell sermon to a congregation of 4000 persons, of whom we were informed there were individuals from every parish in Caithness, from Acts xx. 32. " And now, brethren, I commend you to God and to the word of his grace which is able to build you up, and to give you an inheritance among all them that are fanctified." The parifh minifter was alfo prefent. As it was in general underftood that he had the doctrines we preached in view, when cautioning his people againft their being taught to feparate faith from works, occafion was taken briefly to recapitulate the apoftle's doctrine, and plainly to fhew the abfolute neceffity of completely feparating faith from works *in the important article of a finner's juftification before God.* At the fame time, the fpeaker appealed to thofe who had heard him, whether he had not uniformly infifted upon the abfolute neceffity of works, on the other hand, as the never-failing fruit and evidence of faith, without which, the faith which any man *might fay* he had, would never fave him. Took occafion alfo to refer particularly to the lives and converfations of many of thofe who were fuch ftrenuous advocates for the doctrine of works; and afked, whether the total and open neglect both of perfonal and family religion, afforded them any ground fo greatly to glory in their pretended good works. Finally, told them, that he was pure from their blood, (referring to the difcourfe connected with his text), which he could not have been, had he not faithfully warned them againft the falfe doctrines which he had heard preached to them.

Monday, 25*th September.* Left Thurfo for Wick. Preached on the way at Catchery, parifh of Watten, to about 300 people. Were met by above a dozen of people from Wick, who had provided accommodation for us during our ftay in that place. About 50 people affembled to worfhip in the evening.

Tuefday, 26. Preached to about 400 people, and in the afternoon to about 900. More perfons came to worfhip than could get admittance.

Wednefday, 27. Preached morning and evening

to about 900. The people seemed considerably affected.

Thursday, 28. Preached at Aucorn in the parish of Wick to about 400 persons. Returned to Wick.

Friday, 29. Preached morning and evening to upwards of 1000 persons, being market-day.

Saturday, 30. Preached morning and evening to about 500 each time.

Lord's day, October 1. Preached in the morning to about 2500 people. Heard the minister in the forenoon preach from Math. xxii. 5. "And they made light of it." He represented that men, in becoming Christians, first began to work out their own salvation, and that then God wrought in them, &c. He spoke much of the criminality of such as found fault with ministers, who were, he said, the successors of the apostles, the ambassadors appointed to carry on the treaty of peace between God and man! In the afternoon, preached to about 4000 people, and took notice of what appeared contrary to the gospel in the minister's sermon, himself being present.

Monday, 2. Preached at Borrowstoun in the parish of Wick, to between 300 and 400 people.

Tuesday and Wednesday, 3 and 4. Preached at Wick morning and evening, each day, congregations from 300 to 400 each time.

Thursday, 5. Preached at Frefwick, parish of Canisbay, to between 300 and 400 people. There is in this neighbourhood a small society professing Baptist principles. They had been formed into a church by means of Sir William Sinclair, who lived here, and who preached amongst them for several years. They have been without a pastor, and without the dispensation of divine ordinances, since his death, many years ago. They meet on the Lord's day for reading the Scriptures and for prayer. Those how are now desirous of being baptised, go to Edinburgh for that purpose.

We faw fome of their leading members, who appeared to be godly perfons.

Friday 6. and *Saturday* 7. Preached at Wick, morning and evening, to about 300. Saw a woman under concern of mind.

Lord's day, 8. Preached in the morning to above 2000, and in the evening to above 4000 people. The congregations, as ufual, were very attentive.

Monday, 9. Preached at Bilpfter, a few miles from Wick, to about 300 people. Vifited a woman ill of a fever, and another who had been long confined. In the evening, he who had been indifpofed, arrived from Thurfo, greatly recovered.

He had preached at Thurfo, on Lord's day, October the 1ft, to from 3000 to 4000 perfons. In the evening there were fuppofed to be near 200 perfons, within doors and without, at family-worfhip. In confequence of the exertions of this day, he was again confined till the Thurfday following, when by the goodnefs of God, he was much relieved, and enabled to walk to the Antiburgher meeting-houfe, where he preached on that, and the two following days. On Lord's day, October 8. he preached in the yard formerly mentioned, to about 4000 perfons, who were very attentive. Let the lovers of Chrift and of immortal fouls, pray that the word fpoken fo frequently in this place may prove the favour of life unto life to many fouls!

We cannot take leave of Thurfo without expreffing our grateful fenfe of the divine goodnefs towards us, in the affectionate conduct of the gentleman and his family with whom we refided. May the Lord recompenfe their kindnefs by beftowing on them bleffings which perifh not in the ufing!

It becomes us alfo to mention, with much thankfulnefs, the Chriftian behaviour of our Antiburgher brethren here, as in other places of the North. May

G

their faith and love abound yet more and more, and may the Spirit with which they are animated be more extenfively diffufed, until the whole of the members of Chrift, fhall be knit together in love, and, as in the days of the apoftles, be of one heart and one foul !

The ftate of religion in Thurfo is very low. We are credibly informed, that this town, containing about 2000 fouls, has not been catechifed thefe forty years. It is not therefore a matter of furprife, that men are here perifhing for lack of knowledge. They have the fcriptures it is true in their own hands, and therefore are without excufe. At the fame time, it is a remark, which, fo far as our obfervation goes, will admit of general application, that where the awful fanctions of God's law, fo ftrongly manifefted in the death of Chrift, are not enforced upon the confciences of finners in the preaching of the gofpel, there, men in general will be found living in a ftate of carelefs fecurity, and faying to themfelves, we fhall have peace, though we walk in the imagination of our own hearts. The Lord however has had a few names here, in the midft of all the careleffnefs which has fo greatly prevailed. The Antiburgher minifter formerly mentioned, laboured in this town for eighteen years, and it is hoped not without effect. There are, befides the members of this congregation, a few individuals who fear God, who, though they were accuftomed chiefly to hear in the Seceffion, did not join their communion, but ftill adhered in this refpect to the eftablifhed Church. The fituation of fuch perfons, calls for much fympathy on the part of their Chriftian brethren. They are expofed to trials peculiarly fevere, of which thofe who live in more favoured fituations can have but fmall conception. May the Lord fanctify to them this ftate of bondage, and may he hear their groanings and fend deliverance

from his holy heaven ! We cannot but efteem it a
token for good from the Lord to this town in general, that the people continued to attend the daily
preaching of the word, during the whole of our ftay.
Were gofpel minifters to be fent into this part of
the country, we think there is reafon to hope, that
a general and abiding concern for the things of eternity would be the confequence.

Wick, Tuefday, 10. Preached in the morning
to about 600, and in the evening to about 700 people.

Wednefday, 11. Left Wick, preached at Clyth
(parifh of Latheron) in our way fouthward to about
700 people. Came forward to the Kirk of Latheron;
but the people not having had intimation, there
were only prefent about 200 of thofe who had heard
in the morning. Came on (feveral friends from
Wick accompanying us) to Dunbeath.

Thurfday, 12. After preaching at Dunbeath
to about 70 perfons, took leave of our friends, and
came forward fame evening to Wilk-houfe, a ftage
upon the road. Saw an elderly woman on the road
at Burrowdale, who lamented much the removal of
two faithful miffionaries, from the Society for propagating Chriftian Knowledge in Scotland, Meffrs
M'Kay and Robertfon, whofe labours appear to
have been bleffed in this neighbourhood. Partly
from fome unhappy difpute, and partly from want
of accommodation, we were forry to underftand,
that there has been no perfon yet appointed to fuc-
ceed the laft of the gentlemen above mentioned,
though it is now three years fince he has been removed to another part of the country.—We are happy
here to ftate, that much good has been done in this,
as well as other parts of this country, by means of
miffionaries and fchoolmafters, employed by this
Society. We met with fome of their fchoolmafters,

and we heard of feveral others, truly pious, and zealous in promoting the knowledge of the gofpel.

Having finifhed the account of our labours in Caithnefs, we fhall here prefent the friends of the truth with fome additional obfervations upon the ftate of the county in general with regard to religion. In all the fhire of Caithnefs, confifting of ten parifhes, we heard of very few inftances of the pure gofpel of Jefus Chrift being faithfully preached. It is the fubject of unfeigned lamentation, that, as in former ages, fo ftill, " the people love to have it fo." It is *their* common language, " It would be well for us, if we could do as we are taught ;" and thus, failing in their attempt of obeying the precept, they yield to the more enfnaring influence of example, and join the multitude in the broad path that leads to deftruction. It is a mournful fact, that it is an univerfal practice in this country, to commute for a fum of money the public profeffion of repentance, enjoined by the Church of Scotland to be made by perfons guilty of adultery or fornication. When fuch perfons have paid the fine, they are admitted to the communion-table, without fcruple. When fuch practices as thefe take place to any extent, no wonder that the land mourn, and that the Lord threaten to vifit us with his fore judgments. " Shall I not vifit for thefe things, faith the Lord?" Nor can it at all furprife thofe who know the gofpel, to learn, that while the name and ordinances of God are thus profaned, men fhould in general be living without God and without Chrift, and confequently without any well-grounded hope in the world. It gives us much pleafure, however, to remark, that the Lord hath not wholly left himfelf without a witnefs, even in thofe places which are moft defolate. It is faid, that in this fhire, about fifty or fixty years ago, the

whole of the minifters were faithful preachers of
Chrift. Their teftimony has been tranfmitted, and
the inftructions and example of humble individuals
have been bleffed of God, for keeping alive a fpirit
of real religion in fome of the interior parts of the
country. It is remarked, that thofe perfons are in
general fuch as live at the greateft diftance from
the churches, and who in confequence meet together by themfelves for the purpofes of religious
conference and worfhip on the Lord's day. They
alfo meet at communion-occafions, when they mu-
tually ftrengthen each other's hands, and encourage
each other's hearts, in the good ways of the Lord.
This chiefly refers to thofe who dwell in the highlands, while in general thofe in the lower parts of the
country appear deftitute of the knowledge even of the
firft principles of religion.—It is alfo with peculiar
fatisfaction we notice fome very pleafing appearances of the divine favour towards the town of Wick.
Within thefe fome years paft, it has pleafed God to
excite in feveral individuals, fome of whom were
formerly living altogether carelefs about religion,
a lively concern for the falvation of their immortal
fouls. They meet together for religious fellowfhip
and prayer, and are earneftly defirous of introducing into the town a ftated gofpel-miniftry. May
the Lord profper them in the work of their hands,
and add to their number many of thofe who are yet
in darknefs and in the fhadow of death !—There is
alfo here an Antiburgher congregation, where it is
hoped the Lord has a people ; but they have been
for fome time in a diftracted ftate by the removal
of minifters, which has probably retarded the pro-
grefs of the gofpel, both in the congregation and
amongft occafional hearers.

Thurfday, October 12. Upon arriving at Wilk-
houfe, in the fhire of Sutherland, we made enquiry

about collecting a congregation, but found that few, if any of the people underſtood the Engliſh lan- guage.

Friday, 13. Came on to Dornoch, the county- town. Heard a melancholy account of the ſtate of religion, and of the doctrines generally taught ; at the ſame time, were comforted to hear of the good that was done at prayer-meetings, which were inſti- tuted in a period when much of the power of god- lineſs was experienced, and are ſtill maintained in many parts of this country. In the neighbourhood of Dornoch, they have a houſe built purpoſely for holding their meetings, which are held once every two or three weeks, and are very numerouſly attended. In other parts of the country, they meet monthly in the pariſh-church. The meetings here referred to are of long ſtanding. Their origin is not well known, but it is thought that they commenced about the time of the revolution. They generally met at firſt in the miniſter's houſe, or in ſome pri- vate houſe in the pariſh. The parochial fellow- ſhip-meetings are now all ſo numerous, that they meet in church. The miniſter acts as moderator. He begins with ſinging, and then prays. In many places, eſpecially if the meeting be thin, he reads a portion of Scripture and explains it. He then aſks if any perſon has a queſtion, or caſe of con- ſcience, to propoſe for the conſideration of thoſe who are to ſpeak at the meeting. A paſſage of Scripture is then mentioned, and a queſtion pro- poſed from it, relative to experimental religion, by ſome perſon preſent. The moderator eluci- dates the paſſage, and ſtates the queſtion as in- telligibly as poſſible. The ſpeakers then deliver their ſentiments with an earneſtneſs ſuited to the importance of the ſubject, and the moderator col- lects their different ideas, corrects any thing that

may be improperly ftated, and gives his own opinion. The man who propofes the queftion never
fpeaks to it. In many places there is a prayer offered up about the middle of the fervice. One of the
fpeakers prays after the fervice is over, and a pfalm is
fung.—Occafions of this nature are highly and de-
fervedly valued by the people. In many places we
underftand they are the chief means of maintaining and carrying forward the work of Chrift.
It is here alfo worthy of particular remark, that
until within thefe few years that fome minifters
have difcountenanced them, it was the practice
of a great part of the North Country to hold
public fellowfhip-meetings on the Friday previous
to the adminiftration of the Lord's fupper. Experienced Chriftians here difcourfed freely of the
manner of the Lord's dealing with them, and were
enabled often to fpeak much to the comfort and
edification of their weaker brethren.

Saturday, 14. Intimation having been fent through
the town the evening before, we preached this morning in the town-houfe to about fixty people. Of
thefe we were told that feveral could not underftand us. We had intended to have fpent the Sabbath here, but as few of the people underftood the
Englifh language, we refolved to go on to Tain,
where we arrived about three o'clock. Sent intimation of fermon, and preached from one of the
ftairs of the church to about 300 people.

Tain, Lord's day, 15. Preached at half paft nine,
to about 450, and in the afternoon, after the difmiffion of the church, to about 500 people. The
people here are highly favoured; they are bleffed
with a zealous and faithful minifter in the Eftablifhed Church, who is the fifth of that character
in immediate fucceffion, and many of them feem
greatly to value their privileges. In the evening we vifited a Sabbath-evening fchool, which has

been lately eftablifhed, and meets in the church. The fchool feems to be in a thriving condition. There are about 100 children who attend. Several of them repeated paffages of the fermons they had heard in the courfe of the day.

Monday, 16. One remained and preached at Tain to about 250 people. The other went forward to Milton, having fent intimation in the morning both to that place and Invergordon. When he arrived at Milton, he found the people engaged in one of the monthly meetings which have been mentioned. The minifter was attending, and one of the people was fpeaking upon a paffage of fcripture in Gaelic, with much apparent animation. Preached to the people after the difmiffion of the meeting. There might be about 200 hearers. Came on to Invergordon, and preached to about 200 people.

Tuefday, 17. One preached at Invergordon in the morning to about 350 perfons. The other went forward, and preached at the village of Drummond to about 200, and afterwards at the town of Dingwall in the ftreet to about 150 perfons. Several Chriftian friends came forward with us from Drummond to Dingwall; among others, one whom it had pleafed God to bring under impreffions of the truth by one of the fermons preached in the ftreet of Invernefs. Since that time a vifible change has taken place in his conduct, and he has attached himfelf to the friends and interefts of the gofpel. May he indeed be redeemed to Chrift from all iniquity, and be kept by his almighty power through faith unto falvation! We might have mentioned other inftances of the power of God apparently accompanying his word in the courfe of our journey, but declined it from our not having had an opportunity of knowing whether the effects were abiding. We have related this inftance, becaufe the change appears fo far to be permanent. To the name of Jefus we would defire to render all the glory of the undeferved honour and happinefs of being inftrumental in plucking any of our fellow-finners as brands out of the burning.

Wednefday, 18. Preached at Dingwall in the Town-houfe to from 250 to 300 perfons. The Hall was quite full. Several of the people appeared very attentive. Came on to Keffock; croffed the ferry, and by the Lord's good hand upon us arrived in fafety at Invernefs in the afternoon, where we had the happinefs to meet our brother whom we had left, in good health. And here we joined in fetting up an Eben-ezer, faying, " Hitherto God hath helped."

Here follows the account of our brother's labours in our abfence.

Auguft 11. After leaving my brethren at Brugh-head, proceeded to Findhorn, where, after intimation, preached in a Relief kirk to about 500 people, who were very attentive, and preffed me much to ftay longer; but this was impracticable, as I meant to be at Invernefs on the Lord's day. Went the fame evening to Forres, and next day proceeded to Invernefs.

Invernefs, Lord's day, 13. Preached on a hill adjoining the town, at 12 o'clock, to about 300 or 400 people, and in the evening to a great concourfe, probably about 2000, who heard with great attention. Intimated fermon for next Sabbath at fame hours.

Wednefday, 16. Preached at Drakies, about two miles diftance from town, to about 100 people, the next day at Auld Dourie, and the day following at Cloughneherry, a few miles from Invernefs, to about 100. The people were very attentive in all thefe places.

Lord's day, 20. Preached on the hill to about 400 at 12 o'clock, and in the evening to a great affembly, as before. Went this week to Dingwall, and preached to about 200 people, who feemed very carelefs, preached alfo at Fairntofh, and at Beuley.

Lord's day, 27. Preached about 8 o'clock on the hill to about 400 people, and in the evening to a crouded affembly, as formerly. Preached this week on the other fide of the river, to about 300 people, who were very attentive. Intimated fermon at Cloughneherry ; but it rained fo much that no congregation could affemble. Vifited two or three families in and near the town, and fpoke with them refpecting the ftate of their fouls. Found the people better informed in the principles of religion than in fome other places.

Lord's day, *3d Septem.* Preached on the hill in the morning to about 300, and in the evening to about 2000 perfons, who were exceedingly attentive. Was prevented preaching in the courfe of the week by indifpofition.

Lord's day, *10th Septem.* Preached this morning in Raining's fchool, for which application had been made on account of the wetnefs of the ground, to about 150 people, and in the evening to much the fame number as formerly. As there was to be a fair in the town this week, intimated fermon for Wednefday evening in the new ftreet. About 150 only attended.

Spent a part of this week in vifiting, with a view to the examination and inftruction of thofe who attended the fermons.

Lord's day, 17. Preached in the morning to about 500 people, and in the evening to a very numerous affembly. Many were much affected during the laft fermon. Found that it was the means in the hand of God, of leading feveral young perfons to difcontinue novel-reading, and walking for amufement on the Sabbath : practices but too common in Invernefs. Was prevented by the rain

from making any excurfion this week. Preached
on the fhore on the Friday evening, where, although
it was exceedingly damp and cold, a confiderable
number of perfons attended.

Lord's day, 24. Preached in the morning to about
400, and in the evening to about 1400 people. A
young man informed me that a perfon at Invergordon was anxious I fhould go there to preach. I
faid that I had not thought of going farther than
Fortrofe, but in confequence of this requeft would
probably vifit Invergordon ; at the fame time I mentioned, that as I had to preach at different places, it was
impoffible to afcertain the day on which I fhould be
there ; that probably it would be the Tuefday or
Wednefday. Left Invernefs for Fortrofe, in a very
heavy rain. Came to Avoch, a fifhing town, on the
fide of the Moray Frith oppofite to Campbelltown,
containing about 400 or 500 people. They are remarked for their decency and fobriety, and their defire of hearing the word of God. Swearing, it is
faid, is by no means fo univerfal a practice here as
it is in fifhing towns in general. Informed about a
dozen of people, that there would be preaching immediately. Began in a fmall field to about eight
or nine perfons ; by the time the prayer was finifhed there were nearly 300, whofe attention and apparent ferioufnefs in hearing fully juftified the ac-
counts given of them. After pronouncing the
bleffing, the people expreffed thankfulnefs, and
urged me to ftay and preach in the morning.
Came on to Fortrofe, where I preached next morning to about 400, who were very attentive. Came
forward to Cromarty, a beautiful fmall town at the
mouth of Cromarty Frith. There is here a confiderable number of inhabitants, and both a Gaelic
and Englifh place of worfhip. Intimated fermon,
and preached to about 300 people near the crofs.
Came on to Inverbreaky, a fcattered village oppo-

fite to Invergordon. Was greatly grieved by learning here, that a number of people had affembled the day before at Invergordon; and had waited from ten in the morning to fix in the evening in expectation of fermon. This was occafioned by the young man formerly mentioned, writing to them, that I pofitively promifed to be there on that day, and that I had ordered him to give intimation at the Kirk-yard gate, which was altogether a miftake. The tide being low, I was informed I could not crofs without waiting three hours. As this would have entirely prevented my preaching that evening, and as I wifhed to be at Invernefs on Saturday, I went forward to Fairntofh. Next morning preached at Dingwall to about 150 people, and in the afternoon to about 120 at Kilbokee, who were very attentive. Came forward in the evening to Invernefs.

Lord's day, October 1. Preached on the hill to about 400 people. A pious minifter, formerly affiftant to Mr Calder of Croy, preached in the neighbourhood (being a remote part of Croy parifh) in a tent, to about 4000 people, who liftened with aftonifhing attention. Preached in the evening to a great concourfe. It began to rain exceffively, but the people, when it was propofed to them to feek fhelter fomewhere, declined it, and remained in the rain, till the fermon was concluded. Went afterwards, and vifited the Sabbath-evening fchools, which were crowded and the people and children very attentive. Two young perfons called to fpeak with me about the ftate of their fouls. From what they faid, it appeared that the Lord was leading them to the knowledge of the truth. Was greatly ftruck upon being accofted by other two young perfons, in the language of the jailor, " Sir, what muft I do to be faved?"

Heard of three young girls, two of them of about twelve, and another about fourteen years of age, who had had a meeting for prayer every evening for some time paſt. Afterwards ſaw them, and exhorted them occaſionally.

Went this week to Invergordon, that the people might not be altogether diſappointed. Arrived there in the afternoon, and preached in the evening to about 200 people, who were very attentive. A number of people attended at family-prayer. Preached in the morning to nearly 300, and then came on to Inverneſs.

Lord's day, 8. Preached in the morning upon the hill to about 200 people. The people remained, though it rained, during the whole of the time. Preached in the evening to a great multitude. A deep and fixed attention was generally diſcovered, and many ſeemed much affected with what they heard.

Went to Campbelltown this week, and preached there four times ſucceſſively to very attentive congregations, generally conſiſting of from 200 to 300. Many of thoſe perſons went to reap the corn at three o'clock in the morning, in order that they might have time to hear the goſpel. May the Lord have afforded to their ſouls that accompanying bleſſing, which alone can render the word profitable to them that hear it.

Inverneſs, Lord's day, October 15. Preached in the morning to from 200 to 300 people. In the evening, preached to a great multitude, whoſe attention was much the ſame as laſt Sabbath.

We are informed, that the power of religion greatly prevailed in this town and neighbourhood for ſeveral generations. The celebrated Mr Bruce, who was in exile here about a hundred and fifty years ago, and who was a faithful and zealous preacher of the goſpel, was inſtrumental in leading multitudes of periſhing ſinners to the knowledge of

H

Jefus Chrift. At that period, the north Highlands of Scotland were in a ftate of greater barbarity than fome of the more civilized parts of Africa are at this day. By the blefling of God, however, on the labours of that good man, and many able and faithful fucceffors, the wildernefs was made to rejoice, and to bloffom as the rofe. But alas! how is the gold become dim, and the moft fine gold changed! The prefent generation, having in general had a religious education, retain the opinions, but have forfaken the practice of their fathers. It is hoped, however, that this knowledge may yet ferve to promote the revival of real religion in this place, if it fhall pleafe God to fend zealous minifters among them, of which many of the people are truly defirous. It is remarkable to obferve the number which flock to hear any of the neighbouring gofpel-minifters, of whom there are feveral, when they come to this place, or its neighbourhood. It is not at all uncommon on fuch occafions to fee three or four thoufand people affemble in the open air to hear the word of life. This ferves to account for what appears at firft view rather furprifing, namely, that a number of young perfons are profpering in religion, in circumftances fo very difadvantageous. There is no parochial vifitation or examination performed by the clergy of this town; but the parifh are in the laudable practice (we fincerely wifh it were general) of paying a catechift, a godly man, who vifits from houfe to houfe, and examines the fervants and lower claffes of people on the Sabbath evenings in fummer. There are fome praying focieties here, which meet weekly, and their members in general travel ten or twelve miles to hear the gofpel. There is an Epifcopal meeting here, over which a bifhop prefides; but religion is much in the fame ftate among them as in the reft of the Scots Epifcopal meetings.

There is also a meeting of Methodists, and a small one of Antiburgher Seceders. By the erection and establishment of the last, it was hoped that the interests of true religion would have been greatly promoted in this quarter; but here it is deeply to be lamented, that zeal for the peculiarities of a party has cut off the prospect of extensive usefulness.

One circumstance is stated as having had a peculiar influence in accelerating the declension of religion in this place, viz. a licence granted on an estate in the neighbourhood for distilling spirits; by which means, many of the lower classes, having the opportunity of gratifying their desire of strong liquor at an easy rate, have fallen into habits of intemperance, than which there can be no vice more hostile to the influence of Christianity. Besides, there is reason to fear, that where distilling prevails, habits of dishonesty are formed by the frauds which are too frequently committed against the revenue.

Inverness, Thursday, 19th October. Sermon delayed in the morning on account of rain. Preached in the evening in New Street to about 300 persons.

Friday, 20th Oct. Preached in the morning to about 300, and in the evening to about 200. Had a meeting of friends afterwards for thanksgiving and prayer.

Saturday, 21. Separated for the Lord's day; one went to Campbelltown and Fort George, another to Nairn, and the third remained at Inverness. In the morning deferred preaching on account of the rain; in the evening preached in the Methodist chapel to from 300 to 400 people.

Inverness, Lord's day, 22. Preached at 8 o'clock in the New Street to about 500 people. Preached in the Methodist chapel in the evening. It was quite full, as well as the minister's house adjoining, besides a great many who stood out of doors. Having heard with regret, that a perfon of deferved repute for piety and evangelical fentiments, had been inculcating it as a duty, that Chriftians fhould hear their parifh-minifters, though they might not preach the gofpel, from the example of our Lord's attending the Jewifh fynagogue; endeavoured at fome length to fhew the contrariety of this advice, to the commandment, 2 John, verfes 10, 11. Heard too, that it had been objected againft our preaching, that we came not in by the door. Afked, whether thofe who made the objection conceived coming in by the door, to mean receiving licenfe, as it is termed, from perfons, many of whom they acknowledged to be the enemies of the crofs of Chrift. Afterwards vifited the Sabbath-evening fchools, which we were happy to find well attended. At worfhip in the Inn, about 50 perfons were prefent.

Lord's day. Preached at Campbelltown in the morning to about 300 people; at Fort George to about 800, who were very attentive; again at Campbelltown in the evening to about 400 perfons. Preached at Nairn from the town-houfe ftair on Saturday evening to about 350 people, and on the Lord's day morning to about 700. Heard fermon in the parifh-church. The text was 2 Pet. i. 6. " And to patience godlinefs." In this fermon, after defcribing godlinefs in feveral particulars, the preacher added, that men were to be faved by faith, repentance and fincere obedience, through the merits and mediation of Jefus Chrift. The atonement of Chrift was not mentioned as the fole bafis of a ftable hope, nor faith as the only principle of acceptable obedience, in any one part of the fermon. Preached in the afternoon, and told the people, that in the fermon preached in the forenoon, the only foundation of true godlinefs, faith in the Lord Jefus Chrift, was, if not omitted, yet entirely mifplaced. That the fum of the doctrine was, that men were to be faved by their own works, in connection with the merits of Chrift ; but that the apoftle ftated a different doctrine, when he argued, that if falvation was by works, then it was no more by grace. Spoke of that repentance by which fome expect to be faved; and endeavoured to fhew how different it was from that godly forrow which worketh repentance unto falvation.

Monday, 23. The two from Invernefs and Campbelltown came on to Nairn. Left it, and went to Auldearn, where we preached to about 800 people, (of whom a great part had come from Nairn). Came on to Forres, where we preached at the crofs, immediately after giving public intimation. Were confiderably difturbed, though not intentionally, in preaching by a band of mufic and drums, but were enabled to fpeak fo as to be heard, and the people, about 400, liftened with much attention. We intended to have ftopped here the night, but being unable to procure beds, were obliged to go on to Elgin, where, by the Divine goodnefs, we arrived in fafety at 9 o'clock. One of our brethren went round, and preached evening and morning at Findhorn to about 400 perfons in the Relief meeting-houfe.

Tuefday, 24. Preached in the morning at Elgin, fame place as formerly, to about 350 perfons, who were very attentive. Left Elgin and came on to Fochabers, arrived at 4 o'clock. Sent public intimation, and preached at 5 to about 150 perfons.

Wednefday, 25. One of us went round by Banff. Preached at Fochabers to about 30 or 40 ; it rained, which was one caufe of the congregation being fo much fmaller than laft evening ; but the total indifference of the people of this place to the concerns of eternity, which has been formerly noticed, muft, at the fame time, not be left out of view. Left Fochabers, and came forward to Keith. Intimated fermon, and preached in the Mafon-lodge

H 3

to about 400 people. Preached in the fame place next morning to about 300. After preaching, one of the Antiburgher feceders came, and expreffed a great defire that there fhould be fome funds raifed to fupport itinerants.

Thurfday, 26. Left Keith, and came on through a very bad road to Huntly. Met with a moft affectionate reception from the Antiburgher brethren in this place. Their fpirit and difpofition towards exertions for fpreading the gofpel both at home and abroad, are manifeft by their addrefs, publifhed in the Miffionary Magazine, Vol. II. page 446. Their conduct to us completely accorded with the expectations we had formed, after hearing from them, and perufing that addrefs. Preached in the Mafon-lodge to nearly 500 people.

Friday, 27. Our brother who had gone to Banff, arrived at Huntly. After leaving Fochabers, he came to Cullen, where he preached to about eleven or twelve people. This place has been formerly noticed for its want of religion. We were informed that there had been but one parochial vifitation within the laft thirty-four years. Went to Portfoy, where being unable to collect a congregation he came forward to Banff; after giving intimation he preached in the Relief meeting to about 150 people. Preached in the fame place on Thurfday morning, then went to M'Duff Town, a village in the neighbourhood, and preached at two o'clock to about 50 perfons; afterwards preached in the evening at the Relief meeting to about 200 hearers: next morning left Banff, and came forward to Huntly.

One went forward and preached at Old Rain to about twenty; another remained and preached at Huntly in the morning to about 600 or 700, and in the evening to about 800 perfons.

The minifter of the Antiburgher congregation

here is esteemed by his people very highly in love for his work's sake. He is abundant in labours, and has been the honoured instrument of doing much good in this part of the country. His congregation, we are informed, are growing in numbers, and in religion, particularly since the formation of the Missionary Society of London, in favour of which they took a decided part at a very early period after its institution. Their exertions in this cause are well known. They have a missionary prayer-meeting, where a number of private Christians associate, which has been very useful in promoting religion in this place. Some persons who at first attended it merely as spectators, and who were entirely careless, have become truly pious, and are now in communion with this church. Even scoffers have become serious, and worship God in their families. These persons ascribe their first religious impressions, to their hearing the prayers that were made at this meeting. The late missionary exertions appear to have this evidence of the divine approbation, that in those places where they are countenanced, religion appears to be revived, and where they are condemned and opposed, religion appears on the decline. They have a Sabbath-evening school at Huntly, consisting of from 100 to 200 children. In the country adjacent, the committee of the Huntly Missionary Society, have lately erected no less han five Sabbath-schools *, and have the hope of erecting several others in different parts. Most of the teachers are members of the above-mentioned committee. Many grown people, who used formerly to mispend the Sabbath, attend in all of them. They behave in general with much decency, and some of them with apparent seriousness. But while these things are going on, Satan is not idle. He appears to be exerting con-

* They are now increased to ten. See Missionary Magazine, No. 20.

fiderable influence in oppofition to this work, not fo much among the thoughtlefs and ignorant, as among thofe profeffing uncommon ftrictnefs in religion. Their religion however appears chiefly to lie in the peculiarities of their profeffion, and in their form of church order. But it is hoped, that the work of God will be carried forward in the midft of every oppofition. There are many Roman Catholics in this neighbourhood. They have chapels at Huntly, Kincardine, Mortlach, and feveral other places. There are alfo feveral Epifcopal Clergymen, and at Huntly and Keith there are focieties of Methodifts, who have been evidently ufeful in reforming the morals of fome of the people.

Saturday, 28. One preached at Inverury, while another went forward to Kintorè; but finding it impracticable to collect a congregation, he did not preach, but went forward to Aberdeen, where we arrived about five in the evening.

Lord's day, 29th *October. Aberdeen.* One preached in the Street, to about 300 or 400 people, while another preached at Gilkomfton to nearly the fame number. Preached in the Old Town upon the difmiffion of the church to about 100 perfons. In the evening one preached in the Relief kirk to about 1400 people, and another in the Gaelic chapel to about 1000.

Monday, 30th *October.* One preached in the morning at Gilkomfton to about 200 people, another in the Relief kirk to about 700. Left Aberdeen about one o'clock; came on to Stonehaven, where we preached in the Mafon-lodge at eight o'clock to about thirty or forty people.

Tuefday, 31ft *October.* Left Stonehaven, came to Bervie, and fent intimation of fermon; but no perfons affembling, we proceeded to Montrofe. Preached in the Burgher meeting, to about 300 people. Spent the evening with fome Chriftian friends, and were happy to find, that two Sabbath-evening fchools had been erected, fince we were there laft, and that they were about to form themfelves into a Society for promoting the eftablifhment of others. We were happy to find, that Mr K——— the Burgher minifter, had begun to preach in fome parts of this neighbourhood ; an example which we hope will be followed by his brethren in other parts of the country.

Wednefday, Nov. 1. Preached in the fame meeting in the morning to about 200. Left Montrofe, and came to Brechin. Preached in the Methodift meeting to about 300 people.

Thurfday, Nov. 2. Preached in the morning in the fame place to about 160 perfons. One of the minifters of the town, with whom we were unacquainted, came up to us after fermon, and heartily bade us God fpeed. Left Brechin, and proceeded to Forfar, where we preached the fame evening to about 200 perfons.

Friday, Nov. 3. Preached in the morning to from thirty to forty perfons. Left Forfar, and came to Glamis. Preached to about 100 people, who were very attentive, and then came forward to Cupar.

Saturday, Nov. 4. After public intimation preached in the Mafon-lodge to about fifty people. One of us then went to Kirrymuir to fpend the Sabbath. Preached in the fame place in the evening to about 200 people.

Lord's day, Nov. 4. Preached at Cupar to about 300 people in the morning, and to about 400 in the evening.

At Kirrymuir, Lord's day. Preached to about 400 people at nine o'clock. Preached again at noon to about 500 perfons. Many were obliged to go away as the place was quite full. The people were very attentive. Returned on Monday to Cupar.

Monday, Nov. 6. Left Cupar for Perth. When

we arrived there, we applied for the Relief church, which was kindly and readily granted. Sent public intimation, and preached at fix o'clock to a congregation of from 500 to 600 people.

Tuesday, Nov. 7. Left Perth and came to Auchterarder. Preached here in the School-houfe to about 300 perfons, and then came forward to a friend's houfe in the neighbourhood of Stirling, one of us being much indifpofed by a fore throat in confequence of the fatigue of much fpeaking. In this too, the condefcenfion and goodnefs of God were ftrikingly difplayed, inafmuch, as that, though he had had frequent attacks of this complaint in the courfe of the journey, he had never been once difabled by its violence from preaching, till he had fully completed the circuit which had been intended.

Having finifhed the narrative of our journey, we beg leave to fubmit a few obfervations to the confideration of thofe who love the Lord Jefus Chrift in fincerity.

From the foregoing account, it appears, that the condition in which multitudes of our countrymen are placed is truly deplorable. With the Scriptures in their hands, they are perifhing for lack of knowledge : nay, they are taught to put their truft in refuges of lies, which the hail fhall fweep away in the day of God's wrath. Surely their miferable circumftances are now proclaiming in the ears of all who know the worth of a Saviour and of immortal fouls, " Come over and help us."—It has been faid, with fome degree of juftice, that Chriftians have of late been more concerned for the falvation of the heathen, than for that of their own countrymen. This, however, let it be remarked, has been in fome meafure owing to ignorance. While their attention has been particularly directed to the Heathen, and their compaffion excited in their

behalf, by every argument which could affect the
minds of Chriftians, the miferable condition of many parts of their own country has feldom been
brought under their review. Many of them may
plead, with truth, "Behold we knew it not." Such
can plead fo no longer: the wretched circumftances of their brethren are now laid before them.
Let thofe then who are animated with love to the
fouls of men give ear to the voice of their mifery,
and haften to pour into their fouls the confolations
of the gofpel. Let them alfo lift up their voice as
a trumpet to warn thofe who are going on fecure in
fins, and by every means endeavour to pluck finners
as brands out of the burning. This is the indifpenfible duty of every Chriftian, according to the
meafure of his ability, of whatfoever kind it be,
and it neceffarily flows from the fecond great commandment, "Thou fhalt love thy neighbour as thyfelf." If thou feeft thy brother drawn unto death,
and do not exert thyfelf for his relief, fhall not he
who pondereth the heart confider it, and fhall he not
render to every one according to his works?

From the foregoing account, it will appear, that
there is much encouragement to exertion. The people, almoft in every place, feem willing to receive,
and thankful for inftruction. The fields are
truly white to harveft. Let Chriftians then, not
only pray, but fhew that their prayers are fincere,
by ufing means to fend forth labourers into this
harveft. In difcharging fo important a duty, they
fhall not only yield obedience to the commandment
of God, who will have all men, all claffes and de-
fcriptions of men, to be faved, but they fhall alfo
render the moft effential fervice to their country.
Thofe who believe the word of God know, that fo
long as men are ftrangers to the gofpel of Chrift,
their minds being wholly earthly and carnal, they
are reftlefs and diffatisfied, and ready, upon the firft

occasion, when dazzling and seducing objects are presented to their view, to rush upon the commission of crimes, from which humanity shrinks back with horror. Influenced, however, by the doctrines of the gospel, the lion becomes a lamb, and those who in times past were almost continually in all evil, become ready to every good word and work. They are now taught effectually to deny all ungodliness; and, seeking to promote the welfare of all around them, to live soberly, righteously, and godly in this present evil world. However much therefore the doctrines of the gospel may be opposed by some and despised by others, yet it is plain to those who know their excellence, that the peace and welfare of society are intimately connected with their propagation; and that it can only be in proportion to the extent of their influence, that any real security can be enjoyed for the good conduct of the subjects of any state. Let this consideration then strengthen the obligations that have been already mentioned; and whatever be the charges, which men, careless of their own souls, and the souls of others, bring against those who exert themselves in this good work, let them go steadily forward in the prosecution of so important an object, conscious of being influenced by no other motive than that of sincere regard both to the present and future interests of their fellowmen.

We shall just state, in concluding these remarks, that there are no means which appear more calculated to promote the dissemination of religious truth than those which have been so successfully employed of late in many parts of the country; we mean the institution of Sabbath-evening schools. * Upon the plan on which these are conducted, they are attended with little or no expence. It is by no

* A full account of the plan upon which the Sabbath-schools are conducted, was published in the Missionary Magazine for May 1797.

means neceſſary, that a man ſhould be a profeſſed teacher.in order to undertake the management of one of them. If he have a.competent acquaintance with the doctrine of ſcripture, and an unfeigned love to immortal ſouls, there is no hazard of his failing in an undertaking of this nature. The greater part of the ſchools lately erected, are taught *gratis* by private Chriſtians, who have come forward in this buſineſs with the moſt praiſe-worthy and exemplary zeal. Let their conduct provoke others in different parts of the country, to ſimilar exertions. By the multiplication of ſuch ſeminaries the moſt important advantages may be expected to be derived to ſociety. Surely the Lord will bleſs the united exertions of his people ; and the riſing generation, inſtructed in their early years in the knowledge of Chriſt, ſhall riſe up, a ſeed to ſerve him ; whoſe labours, in their turn, may prove the happy means of effecting a general reformation on public manners, and of extending the knowledge of Chriſt's ſalvation to the uttermoſt ends of the earth.

THE END.

Part 56.]   NEW SERIES.   [Sixpence.

little

AUGUST, 1879.

FRONTISPIECE—"A Perilous Moment."

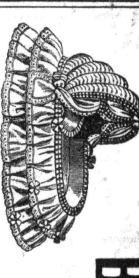